SRA
Connecting
Math Concepts

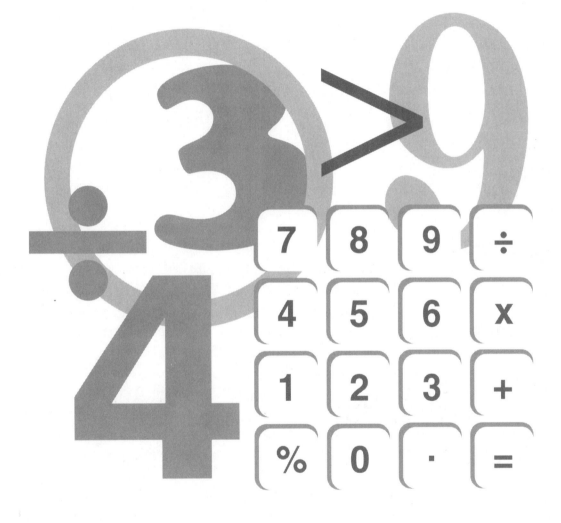

Columbus, Ohio

The **McGraw·Hill** Companies

www.sra4kids.com

 **SRA
McGraw-Hill**

Send all inquiries to:
SRA/McGraw-Hill
4400 Easton Commons
Columbus, OH 43219

Printed in the United States of America.

ISBN 0-02-684655-1

10 11 DBH 10 09 08

Lesson A

a. A penny is worth 1 cent.

b. A nickel is worth 5 cents.

c. A dime is worth 10 cents.

d. A quarter is worth 25 cents.

a. $5 + 4 =$ ⬚   c. $7 - 2 =$ ⬚   e. $7 + 3 =$ ⬚

b. $5 - 4 =$ ⬚   d. $7 + 2 =$ ⬚   f. $7 - 3 =$ ⬚

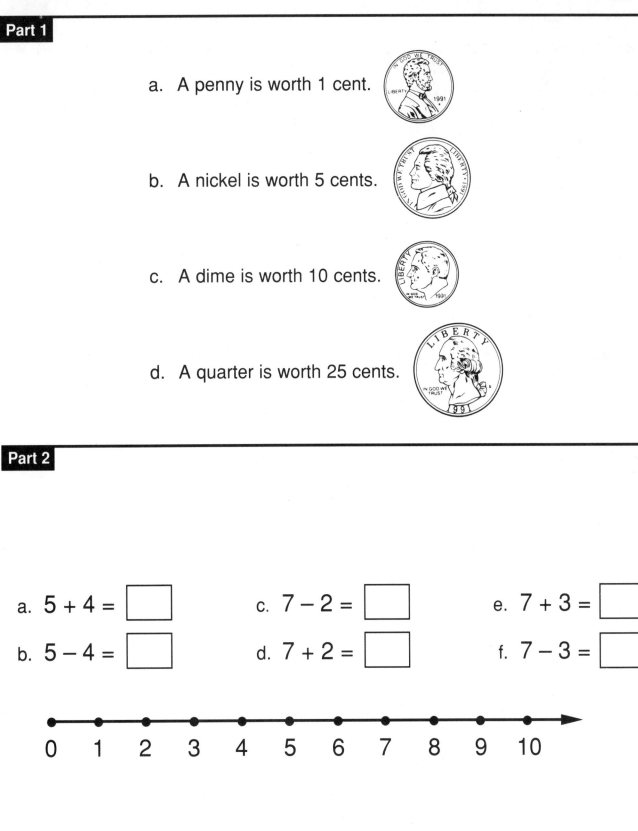

0   1   2   3   4   5   6   7   8   9   10

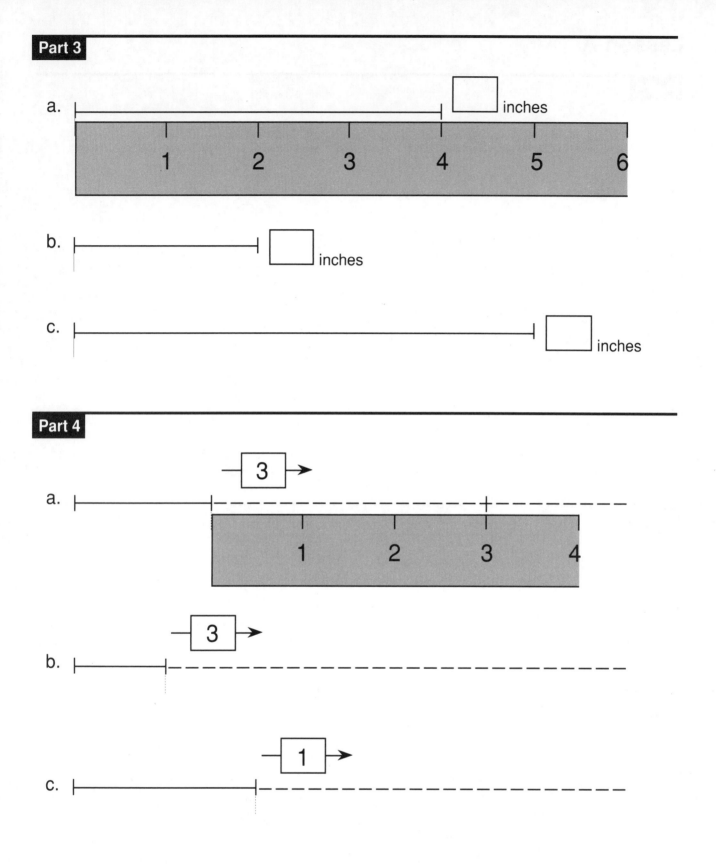

Lesson B

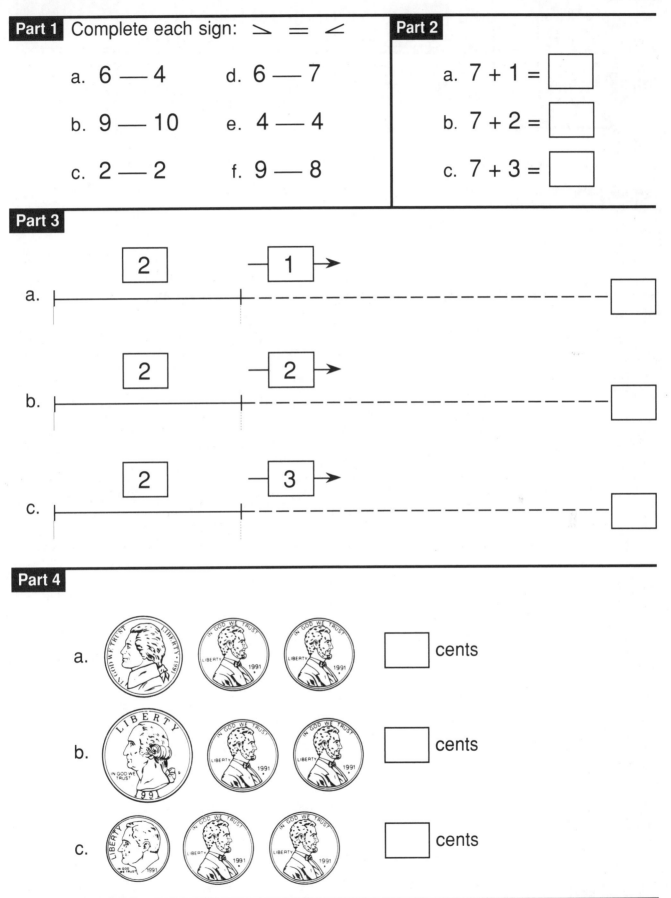

Part 1 Complete each sign: $>$ $=$ $<$

a. 6 — 4   d. 6 — 7

b. 9 — 10   e. 4 — 4

c. 2 — 2   f. 9 — 8

Part 2

a. 7 + 1 = ☐

b. 7 + 2 = ☐

c. 7 + 3 = ☐

Part 3

a. |2| →|1|→ ☐

b. |2| →|2|→ ☐

c. |2| →|3|→ ☐

Part 4

a. ☐ cents

b. ☐ cents

c. ☐ cents

3

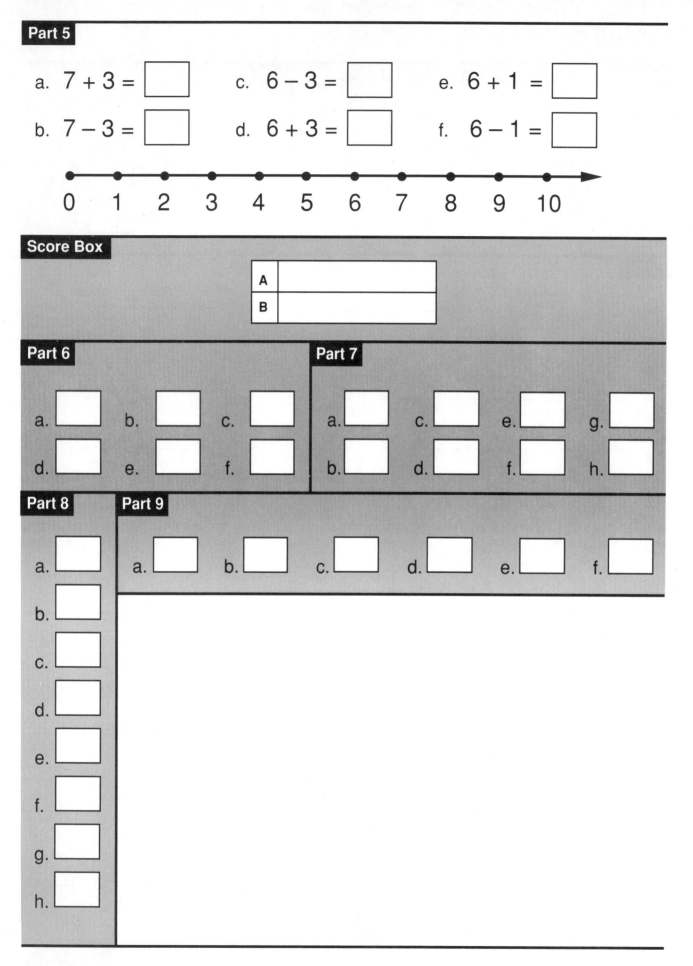

Part 5

a. 7 + 3 = ☐   c. 6 − 3 = ☐   e. 6 + 1 = ☐

b. 7 − 3 = ☐   d. 6 + 3 = ☐   f. 6 − 1 = ☐

0   1   2   3   4   5   6   7   8   9   10

Score Box

A	
B	

Part 6

a. ☐   b. ☐   c. ☐

d. ☐   e. ☐   f. ☐

Part 7

a. ☐   c. ☐   e. ☐   g. ☐

b. ☐   d. ☐   f. ☐   h. ☐

Part 8

a. ☐

b. ☐

c. ☐

d. ☐

e. ☐

f. ☐

g. ☐

h. ☐

Part 9

a. ☐   b. ☐   c. ☐   d. ☐   e. ☐   f. ☐

Lesson 1

Part 1

a.   b.   c.

d.   e.   f.

Part 2

a.   c.   e.

b.   d.   f.

Part 3

a.

b.

c.

d.

e.

Part 4

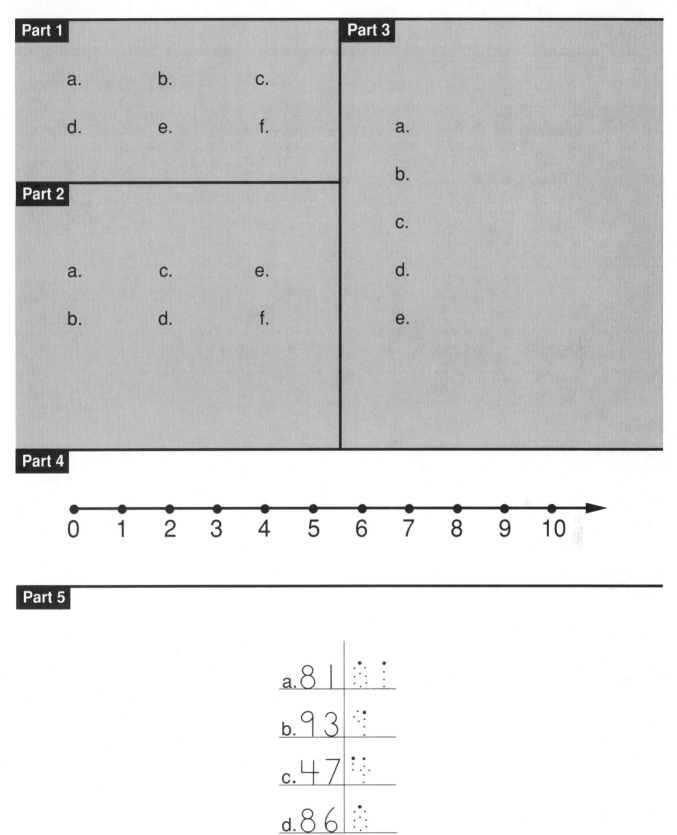

0   1   2   3   4   5   6   7   8   9   10

Part 5

a. 81

b. 93

c. 47

d. 86

Lesson 2

Part 1 Cross out these items:

a in part 4   c in part 2   b in part 3   f in part 4   d in part 3

a. ☐   b. ☐   c. ☐   d. ☐

e. ☐   f. ☐   g. ☐   h. ☐

Part 2

a. ☐   c. ☐   e. ☐   g. ☐

b. ☐   d. ☐   f. ☐   h. ☐

Part 3

a. ☐   e. ☐

b. ☐   f. ☐

c. ☐   g. ☐

d. ☐

Part 4

a. ☐   b. ☐   c. ☐

d. ☐   e. ☐   f. ☐

g. ☐   h. ☐   i. ☐

Part 5

0   1   2   3   4   5   6   7   8   9   10

Part 6

a. ____

b. ____

c. ____

d. ____

Part 7

a. $3 + 5 =$ ☐

b. $6 + 4 =$ ☐

c. $5 + 3 =$ ☐

Part 8

a. 9 8

b. 4 9

c. 8 2

Lesson 3

Part 1 **Cross out these items:**
f in part 4   a in part 3   b in part 1
d in part 1   b in part 2   e in part 4

a. ☐   c. ☐   e. ☐   g. ☐

b. ☐   d. ☐   f. ☐   h. ☐

Part 2

a. ☐   b. ☐   c. ☐

d. ☐   e. ☐   f. ☐

Part 3

a. ☐   d. ☐   g. ☐

b. ☐   e. ☐   h. ☐

c. ☐   f. ☐   i. ☐

Part 4

a. ☐

b. ☐

c. ☐

d. ☐

e. ☐

f. ☐

Part 5

a. $6 + 4 =$ ☐   c. $5 + 4 =$ ☐

b. $6 + 2 =$ ☐   d. $7 + 1 =$ ☐

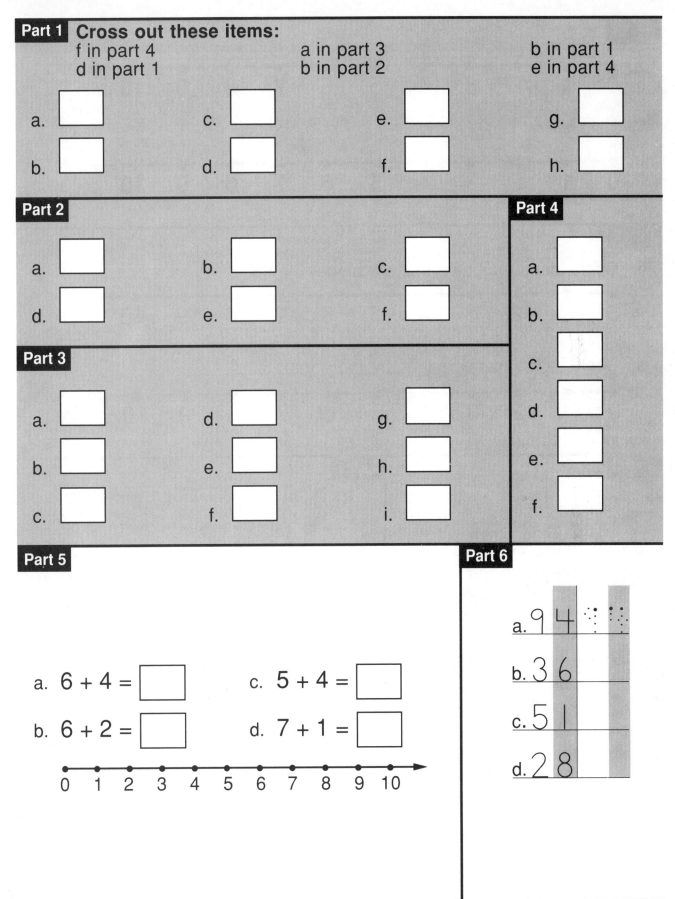

0 1 2 3 4 5 6 7 8 9 10

Part 6

a. 9 4

b. 3 6

c. 5 1

d. 2 8

Lesson 4

Part 1

a.
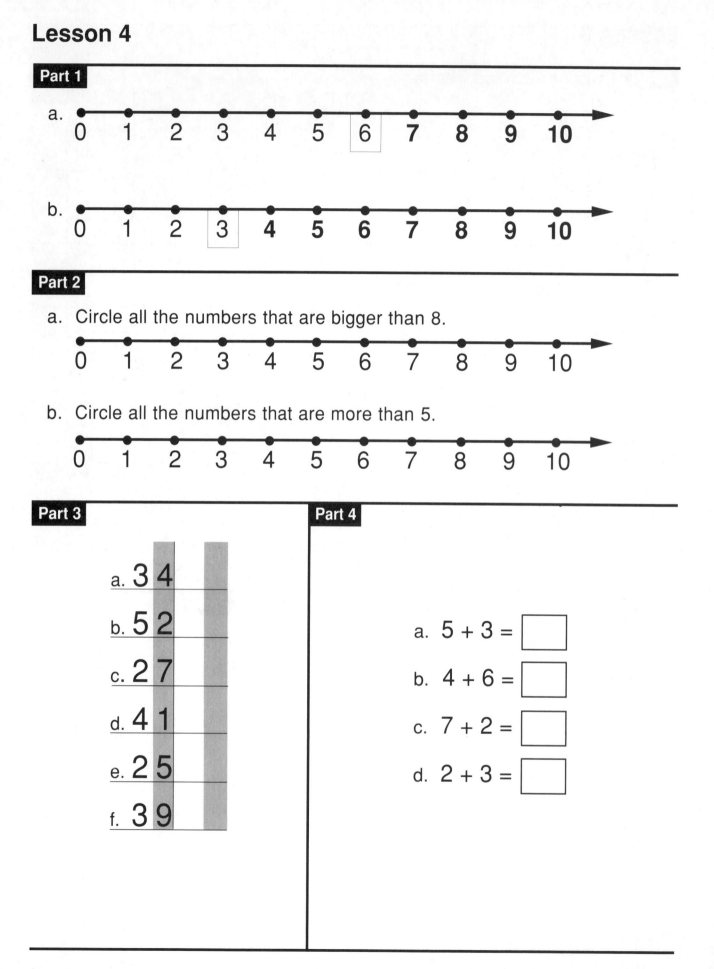
0　1　2　3　4　5　6　7　8　9　10

b.
0　1　2　3　4　5　6　7　8　9　10

Part 2

a. Circle all the numbers that are bigger than 8.

0　1　2　3　4　5　6　7　8　9　10

b. Circle all the numbers that are more than 5.

0　1　2　3　4　5　6　7　8　9　10

Part 3

a. 3 4

b. 5 2

c. 2 7

d. 4 1

e. 2 5

f. 3 9

Part 4

a. 5 + 3 = ☐

b. 4 + 6 = ☐

c. 7 + 2 = ☐

d. 2 + 3 = ☐

Score Box

A	
B	

Part 5

a. ☐   b. ☐   c. ☐   d. ☐

e. ☐   f. ☐   g. ☐   h. ☐

Part 6

a. ☐   c. ☐   e. ☐   g. ☐

b. ☐   d. ☐   f. ☐   h. ☐

Part 7

a. ☐

b. ☐

c. ☐

d. ☐

e. ☐

f. ☐

g. ☐

Part 8

a. ☐   b. ☐   c. ☐

d. ☐   e. ☐   f. ☐

g. ☐   h. ☐   i. ☐

Lesson 5

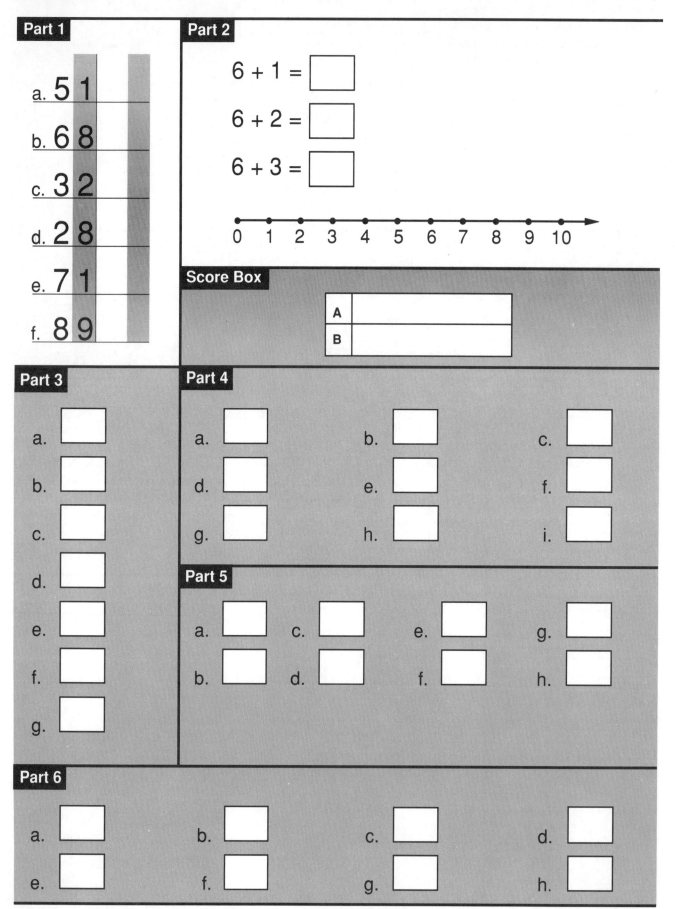

Part 1

a. 5 1

b. 6 8

c. 3 2

d. 2 8

e. 7 1

f. 8 9

Part 2

6 + 1 = ☐

6 + 2 = ☐

6 + 3 = ☐

0 1 2 3 4 5 6 7 8 9 10

Score Box

A	
B	

Part 3

a. ☐

b. ☐

c. ☐

d. ☐

e. ☐

f. ☐

g. ☐

Part 4

a. ☐   b. ☐   c. ☐

d. ☐   e. ☐   f. ☐

g. ☐   h. ☐   i. ☐

Part 5

a. ☐   c. ☐   e. ☐   g. ☐

b. ☐   d. ☐   f. ☐   h. ☐

Part 6

a. ☐   b. ☐   c. ☐   d. ☐

e. ☐   f. ☐   g. ☐   h. ☐

a. Circle all the numbers that are more than 7.

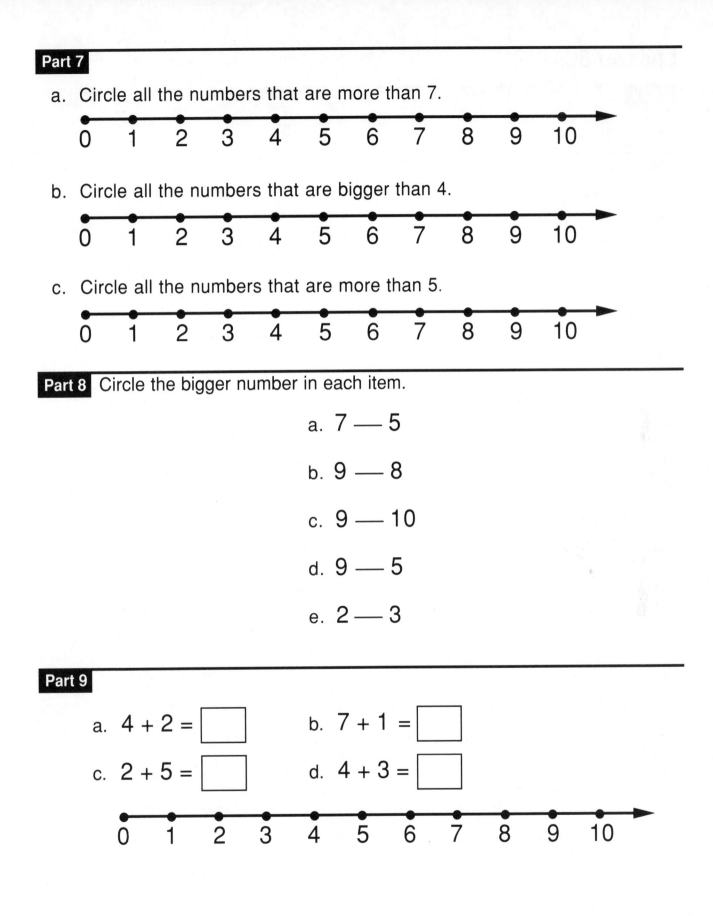

0 1 2 3 4 5 6 7 8 9 10

b. Circle all the numbers that are bigger than 4.

0 1 2 3 4 5 6 7 8 9 10

c. Circle all the numbers that are more than 5.

0 1 2 3 4 5 6 7 8 9 10

Part 8 Circle the bigger number in each item.

a. 7 — 5

b. 9 — 8

c. 9 — 10

d. 9 — 5

e. 2 — 3

Part 9

a. 4 + 2 = ☐   b. 7 + 1 = ☐

c. 2 + 5 = ☐   d. 4 + 3 = ☐

0 1 2 3 4 5 6 7 8 9 10

Lesson 6

Part 1

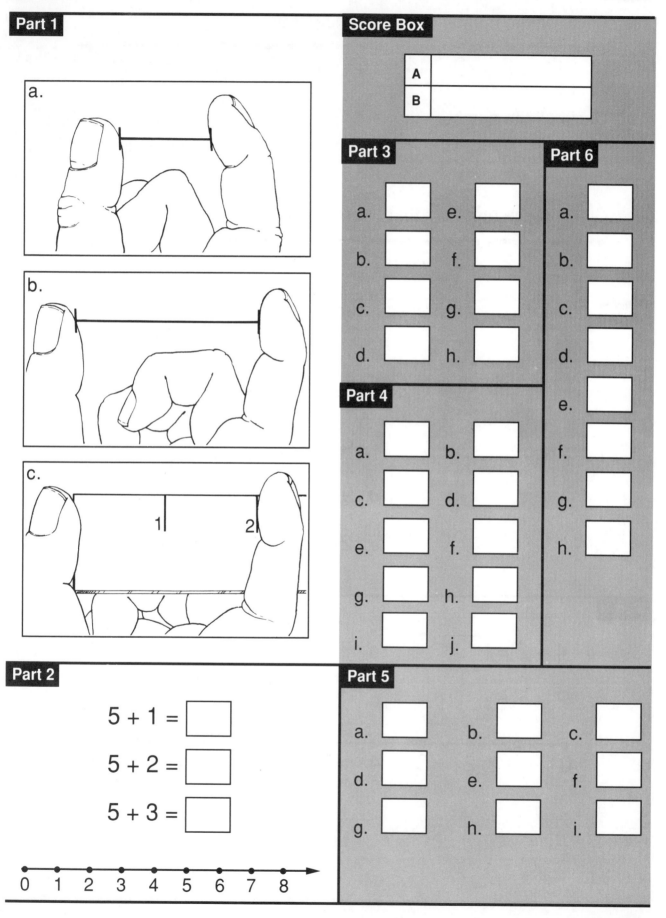

a.

b.

c.

1   2

Part 2

5 + 1 = ☐

5 + 2 = ☐

5 + 3 = ☐

0 1 2 3 4 5 6 7 8

Score Box

A	
B	

Part 3

a. ☐   e. ☐
b. ☐   f. ☐
c. ☐   g. ☐
d. ☐   h. ☐

Part 4

a. ☐   b. ☐
c. ☐   d. ☐
e. ☐   f. ☐
g. ☐   h. ☐
i. ☐   j. ☐

Part 5

a. ☐   b. ☐   c. ☐
d. ☐   e. ☐   f. ☐
g. ☐   h. ☐   i. ☐

Part 6

a. ☐
b. ☐
c. ☐
d. ☐
e. ☐
f. ☐
g. ☐
h. ☐

a. Circle all the numbers that are more than 7.

0 1 2 3 4 5 6 7 8 9 10

b. Circle all the numbers that are bigger than 3.

0 1 2 3 4 5 6 7 8 9 10

c. Circle all the numbers that are more than 5.

0 1 2 3 4 5 6 7 8 9 10

Part 8 Circle the bigger number in each item. **Part 9**

a. 3 — 4

b. 9 — 7

c. 5 — 4

d. 8 — 10

e. 1 — 2

a. 2 7

b. 5 6

c. 3 1

d. 5 1

e. 8 3

f. 2 2

Lesson 7

Part 1

a. ├────────┤

b. ├──────────────┤

Part 2

a. $5 + 1 = \boxed{}$ d. $5 + 2 = \boxed{}$

b. $5 + 2 = \boxed{}$ e. $5 + 1 = \boxed{}$

c. $5 + 3 = \boxed{}$ f. $5 + 3 = \boxed{}$

0 1 2 3 4 5 6 7 8 9 10

Part 3

a. 3 ■ 5 ■ 1

b. 6 ■ 3 ■ 2

c. 6 ■ 2 ■ 5

d. 4 ■ 6 ■ 2

Part 4

a. _____

b. _____

c. _____

d. _____

e. _____

Lesson 8

Part 1

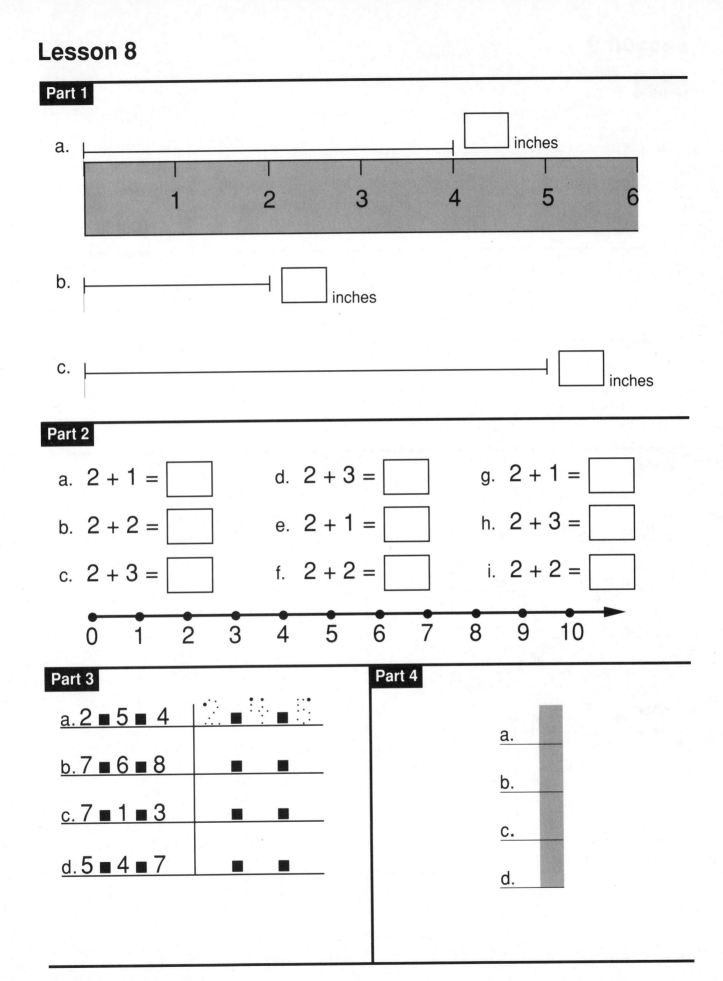

a. [ ] inches

b. [ ] inches

c. [ ] inches

Part 2

a. 2 + 1 = [ ]

b. 2 + 2 = [ ]

c. 2 + 3 = [ ]

d. 2 + 3 = [ ]

e. 2 + 1 = [ ]

f. 2 + 2 = [ ]

g. 2 + 1 = [ ]

h. 2 + 3 = [ ]

i. 2 + 2 = [ ]

0 1 2 3 4 5 6 7 8 9 10

Part 3

a. 2 ■ 5 ■ 4

b. 7 ■ 6 ■ 8

c. 7 ■ 1 ■ 3

d. 5 ■ 4 ■ 7

Part 4

a.

b.

c.

d.

Lesson 9

Part 1

a. ├──────────────────────────────────────┤ ☐
inches

b. ├──┤ ☐
inches

c. ├────────────────────────┤ ☐
inches

Part 2

a. 5 ■ 4 ■ 7 │ ■　　■

b. 3 ■ 6 ■ 1 │ ■　　■

c. 5 ■ 3 ■ 4 │ ■　　■

d. 4 ■ 7 ■ 8 │ ■　　■

Part 3

a.

b.

c.

d.

Score Box

A	
B	

Part 4

a. ☐
b. ☐

c. ☐
d. ☐

e. ☐
f. ☐

g. ☐
h. ☐

Part 5

a. ☐
b. ☐
c. ☐
d. ☐
e. ☐
f. ☐
g. ☐

Part 6

a. ☐
d. ☐
g. ☐

b. ☐
e. ☐
h. ☐

c. ☐
f. ☐
i. ☐

Part 7

a. ☐
e. ☐

b. ☐
f. ☐

c. ☐
g. ☐

d. ☐
h. ☐

Part 8

a. $3 + 1 =$ ☐

b. $3 + 2 =$ ☐

c. $3 + 3 =$ ☐

d. $3 + 1 =$ ☐

e. $3 + 3 =$ ☐

f. $3 + 2 =$ ☐

g. $3 + 3 =$ ☐

h. $3 + 1 =$ ☐

```
0   1   2   3   4   5   6   7   8   9   10
```

Lesson 10

Part 1

a. How long is line **a?**

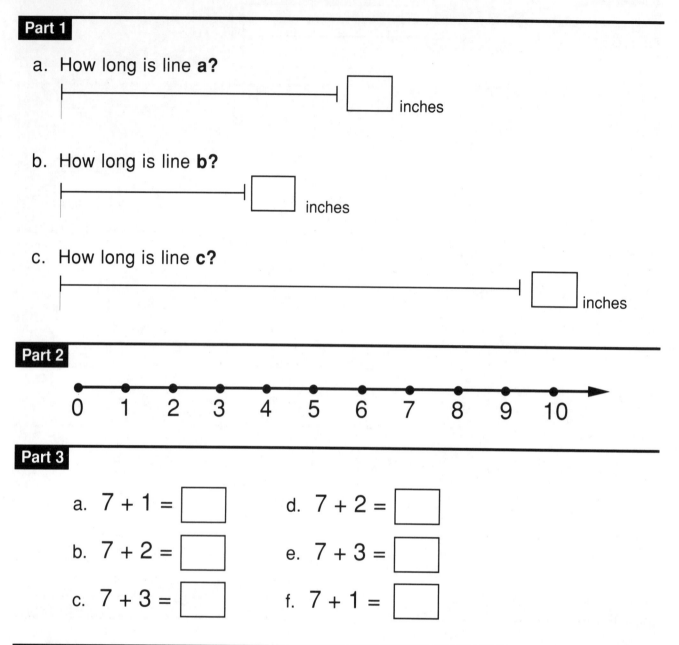

☐ inches

b. How long is line **b?**

☐ inches

c. How long is line **c?**

☐ inches

Part 2

0   1   2   3   4   5   6   7   8   9   10

Part 3

a. 7 + 1 = ☐   d. 7 + 2 = ☐

b. 7 + 2 = ☐   e. 7 + 3 = ☐

c. 7 + 3 = ☐   f. 7 + 1 = ☐

Part 4 Write the smallest number first. Then write the middle-sized number. Then write the biggest number.

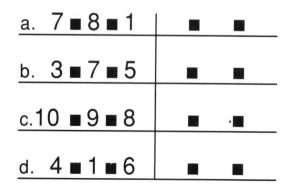

a. 7 ■ 8 ■ 1   ■   ■

b. 3 ■ 7 ■ 5   ■   ■

c. 10 ■ 9 ■ 8   ■   ■

d. 4 ■ 1 ■ 6   ■   ■

Test 1

Part 1

a. ├─────────────────────────────────────┤ ▢ inches

b. ├───┤ ▢ inches

c. ├────────────────────────────┤ ▢ inches

Part 2

a. $4 + 1 =$ ▢   d. $4 + 3 =$ ▢

b. $4 + 2 =$ ▢   e. $4 + 1 =$ ▢

c. $4 + 3 =$ ▢   f. $4 + 2 =$ ▢

●───●───●───●───●───●───●───●───●───●───►
0   1   2   3   4   5   6   7   8   9   10

Part 3 Write the smallest number first. Then write the middle-sized number. Then write the biggest number.

a. 8 ■ 10 ■ 9 | ■   ■

b. 3 ■ 6 ■ 7 | ■   ■

c. 10 ■ 4 ■ 7 | ■   ■

d. 5 ■ 7 ■ 6 | ■   ■

Test 1/Extra Practice

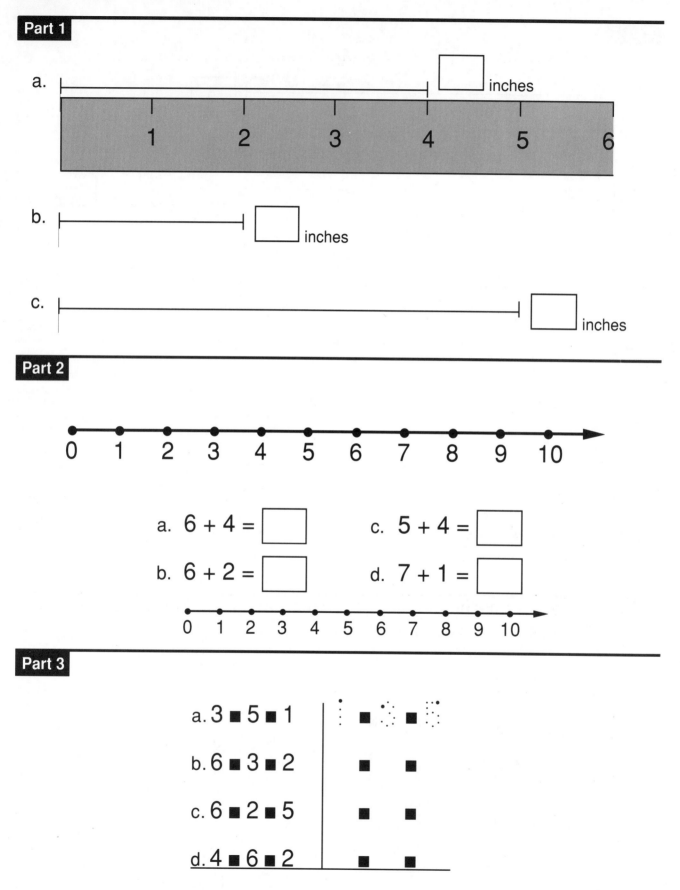

a. ▢ inches

b. ▢ inches

c. ▢ inches

Part 2

a. 6 + 4 = ▢   c. 5 + 4 = ▢

b. 6 + 2 = ▢   d. 7 + 1 = ▢

Part 3

a. 3 ■ 5 ■ 1

b. 6 ■ 3 ■ 2

c. 6 ■ 2 ■ 5

d. 4 ■ 6 ■ 2

Lesson 11

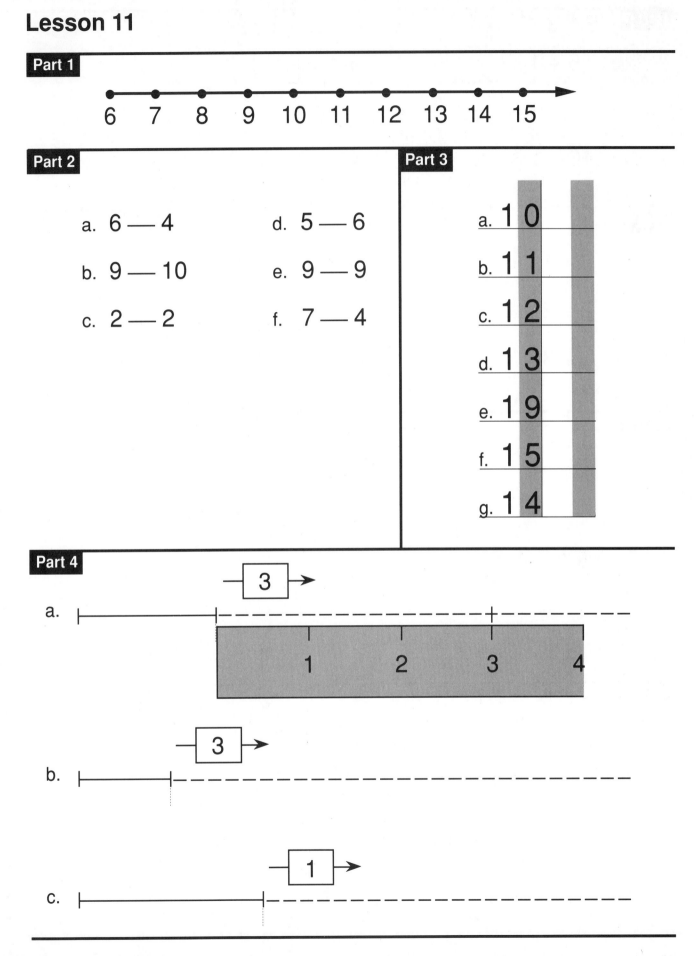

Part 1

6 7 8 9 10 11 12 13 14 15

Part 2

a. 6 — 4   d. 5 — 6

b. 9 — 10   e. 9 — 9

c. 2 — 2   f. 7 — 4

Part 3

a. 10

b. 11

c. 12

d. 13

e. 19

f. 15

g. 14

Part 4

a. [3]→

1 2 3 4

b. [3]→

c. [1]→

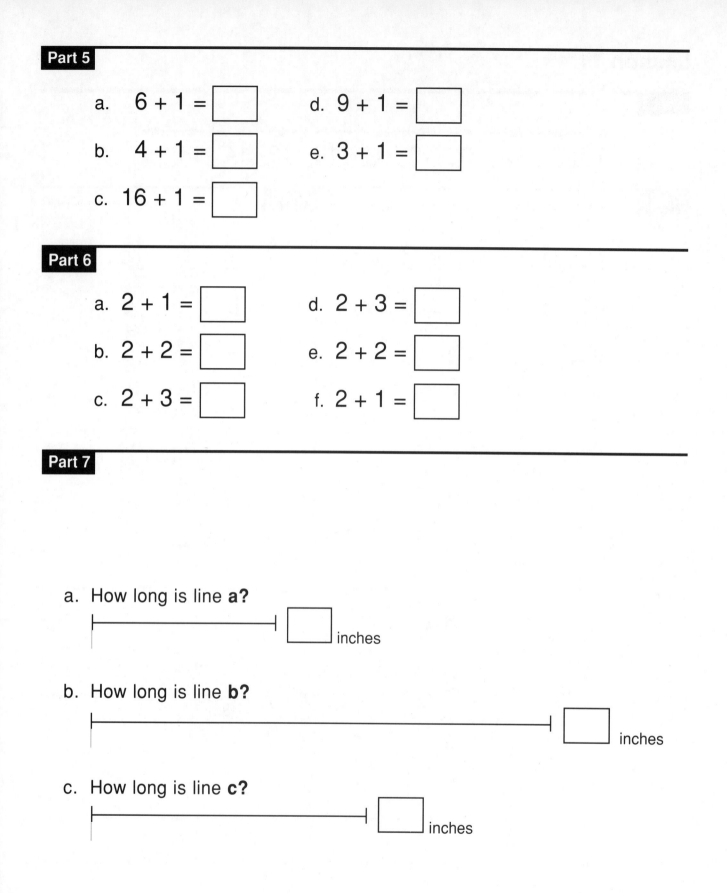

Part 5

a. $6 + 1 = \boxed{}$ d. $9 + 1 = \boxed{}$

b. $4 + 1 = \boxed{}$ e. $3 + 1 = \boxed{}$

c. $16 + 1 = \boxed{}$

Part 6

a. $2 + 1 = \boxed{}$ d. $2 + 3 = \boxed{}$

b. $2 + 2 = \boxed{}$ e. $2 + 2 = \boxed{}$

c. $2 + 3 = \boxed{}$ f. $2 + 1 = \boxed{}$

Part 7

a. How long is line **a?**

$\boxed{}$ inches

b. How long is line **b?**

$\boxed{}$ inches

c. How long is line **c?**

$\boxed{}$ inches

Lesson 12

Part 1

a. $6 - 4 = \boxed{}$ b. $6 - 2 = \boxed{}$ c. $9 - 2 = \boxed{}$

```
0   1   2   3   4   5   6   7   8   9   10
```

Part 2

a. 3 — 7   d. 4 — 5

b. 9 — 9   e. 8 — 5

c. 8 — 6   f. 3 — 3

Part 3

a. $6 + 2 = \boxed{}$

b. $1 + 5 = \boxed{}$

c. $3 + 4 = \boxed{}$

Part 4

a. 17

b. 12

c. 10

d. 13

e. 18

Part 5

a. ──────────── $\boxed{1}$ →

b. ──────── $\boxed{2}$ →

c. ──── $\boxed{3}$ →

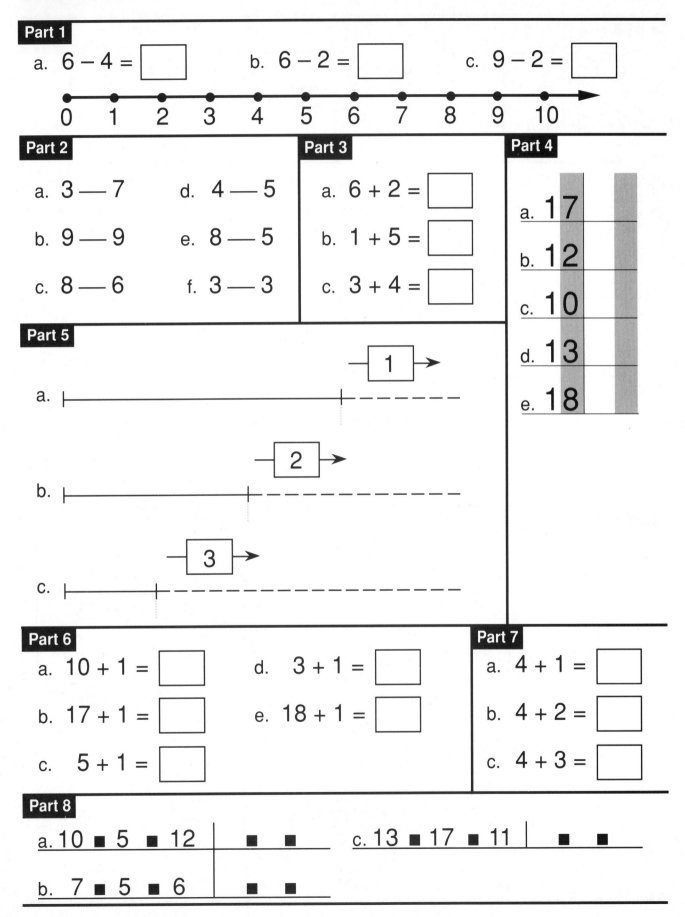

Part 6

a. $10 + 1 = \boxed{}$ d. $3 + 1 = \boxed{}$

b. $17 + 1 = \boxed{}$ e. $18 + 1 = \boxed{}$

c. $5 + 1 = \boxed{}$

Part 7

a. $4 + 1 = \boxed{}$

b. $4 + 2 = \boxed{}$

c. $4 + 3 = \boxed{}$

Part 8

a. 10 ■ 5 ■ 12 | ■ ■   c. 13 ■ 17 ■ 11 | ■ ■

b. 7 ■ 5 ■ 6 | ■ ■

23

Lesson 13

a. $6 - 2 = \boxed{}$ c. $8 - 2 = \boxed{}$ e. $6 - 5 = \boxed{}$

b. $7 - 3 = \boxed{}$ d. $3 - 2 = \boxed{}$

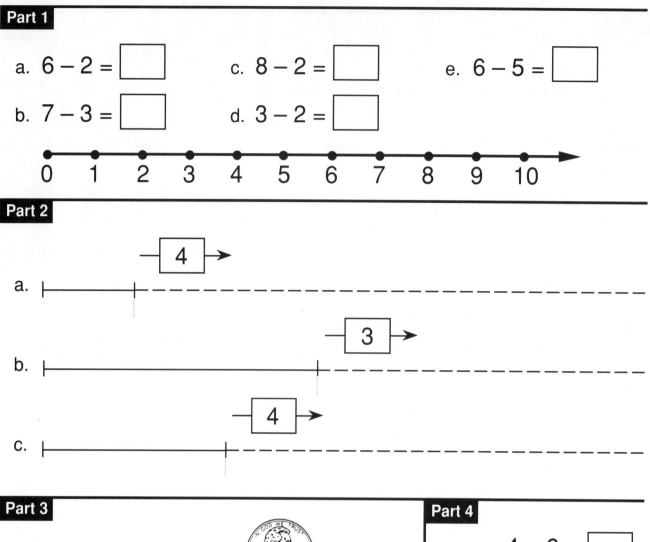

0 1 2 3 4 5 6 7 8 9 10

Part 2

a.

|4|→

b.

|3|→

c.

|4|→

Part 3

a. A penny is worth 1 cent.

b. A nickel is worth 5 cents.

c. A dime is worth 10 cents.

d. A quarter is worth 25 cents.

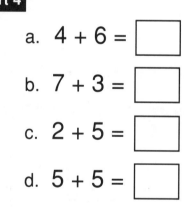

Part 4

a. $4 + 6 = \boxed{}$

b. $7 + 3 = \boxed{}$

c. $2 + 5 = \boxed{}$

d. $5 + 5 = \boxed{}$

Part 5

a. ___ + 1 = ▢

b. ___ + 2 = ▢

c. 8 + 3 = ▢

d. 8 + 2 = ▢

e. 8 + 1 = ▢

f. 8 + 3 = ▢

g. 8 + 2 = ▢

h. 8 + 1 = ▢

Part 6 Write the numerals.

a. 5 1

b. 7 1

c. 1 7

d. 1 3

e. 9 4

f. 1 2

Part 7 Complete each sign: > = <

a. 5 — 1

b. 1 — 5

c. 5 — 5

d. 3 — 4

e. 9 — 10

f. 9 — 9

Part 8

a. 5 + 1 = ▢

b. 8 + 1 = ▢

c. 6 + 1 = ▢

d. 3 + 1 = ▢

e. 7 + 1 = ▢

f. 2 + 1 = ▢

Lesson 14

Part 1

a. $5 + 4 = \boxed{}$ c. $7 - 2 = \boxed{}$

b. $5 - 4 = \boxed{}$ d. $7 + 2 = \boxed{}$

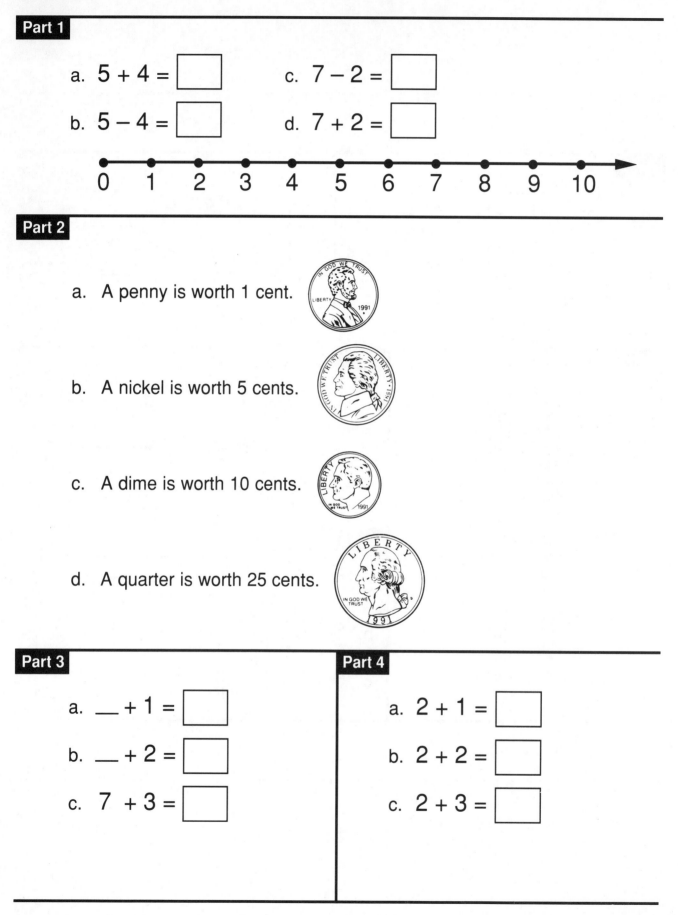

```
0   1   2   3   4   5   6   7   8   9   10
```

Part 2

a. A penny is worth 1 cent.

b. A nickel is worth 5 cents.

c. A dime is worth 10 cents.

d. A quarter is worth 25 cents.

Part 3

a. __ $+ 1 = \boxed{}$

b. __ $+ 2 = \boxed{}$

c. $7 + 3 = \boxed{}$

Part 4

a. $2 + 1 = \boxed{}$

b. $2 + 2 = \boxed{}$

c. $2 + 3 = \boxed{}$

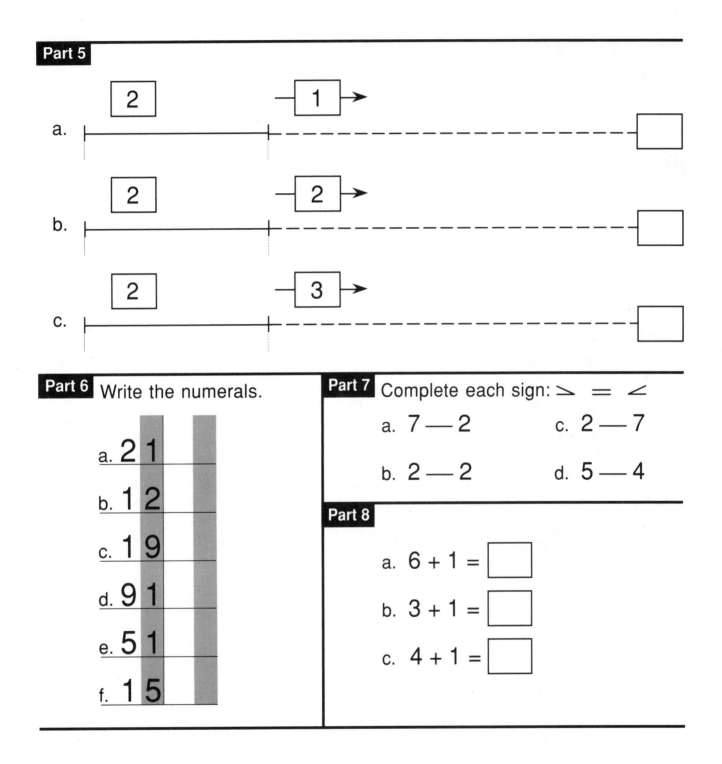

Part 5

a.

2   — 1 →

b.

2   — 2 →

c.

2   — 3 →

Part 6 Write the numerals.

a. 2 1

b. 1 2

c. 1 9

d. 9 1

e. 5 1

f. 1 5

Part 7 Complete each sign: > = <

a. 7 — 2   c. 2 — 7

b. 2 — 2   d. 5 — 4

Part 8

a. 6 + 1 = ☐

b. 3 + 1 = ☐

c. 4 + 1 = ☐

Lesson 15

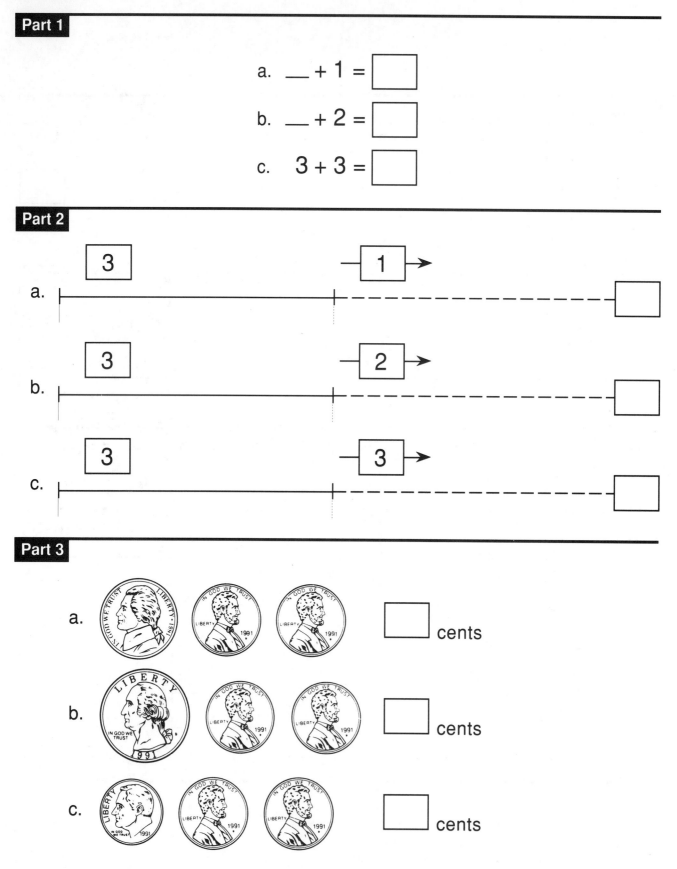

a. __ + 1 = ☐

b. __ + 2 = ☐

c. 3 + 3 = ☐

Part 2

a.

3   1 →

b.

3   2 →

c.

3   3 →

Part 3

a. ☐ cents

b. ☐ cents

c. ☐ cents

Part 4

a. $7 + 3 = \boxed{}$ b. $7 - 3 = \boxed{}$

c. $6 - 3 = \boxed{}$ d. $6 + 3 = \boxed{}$

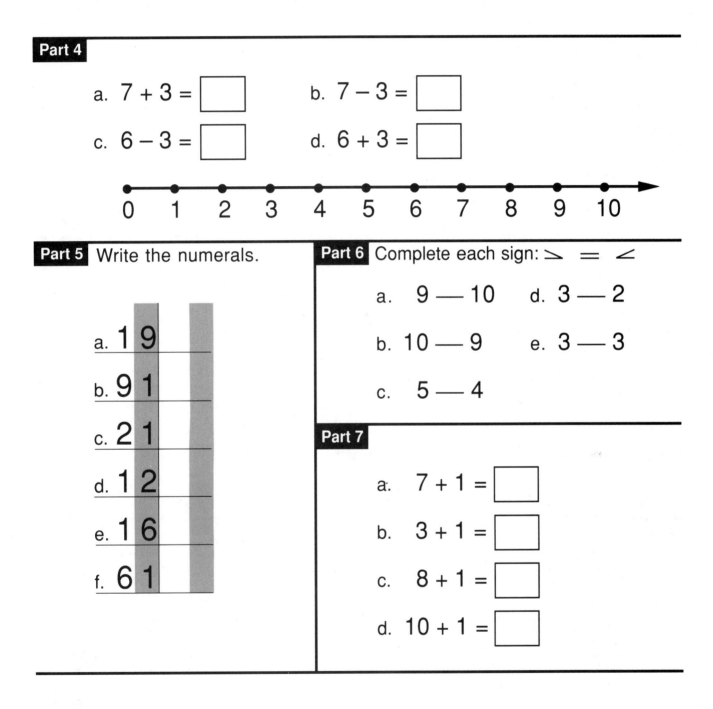

0   1   2   3   4   5   6   7   8   9   10

Part 5 Write the numerals.

a. 1 9 _____

b. 9 1 _____

c. 2 1 _____

d. 1 2 _____

e. 1 6 _____

f. 6 1 _____

Part 6 Complete each sign: $>$ $=$ $<$

a.   9 — 10   d. 3 — 2

b. 10 — 9   e. 3 — 3

c.   5 — 4

Part 7

a. $7 + 1 = \boxed{}$

b. $3 + 1 = \boxed{}$

c. $8 + 1 = \boxed{}$

d. $10 + 1 = \boxed{}$

Lesson 16

a.  ☐ cents

b. ☐ cents

c. ☐ cents

Part 2

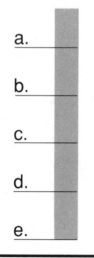

a. _____

b. _____

c. _____

d. _____

e. _____

Part 3

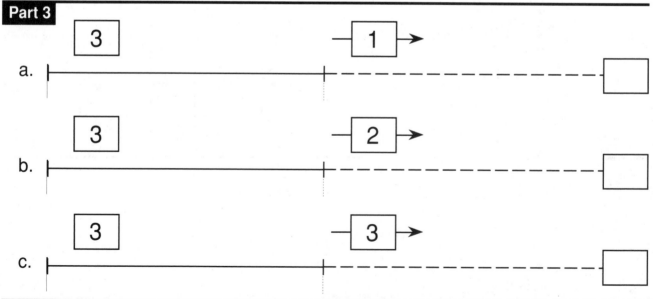

a. $\boxed{3}$ → $\boxed{1}$ → ☐

b. $\boxed{3}$ → $\boxed{2}$ → ☐

c. $\boxed{3}$ → $\boxed{3}$ → ☐

A	
B	

a. 7 + 1 = 8

7 + 2 = ☐

b. 5 + 1 = 6

5 + 2 = ☐

c. 3 + 1 = 4

3 + 2 = ☐

d. 9 + 1 = 10

9 + 2 = ☐

e. 10 + 1 = 11

10 + 2 = ☐

f. 4 + 1 = 5

4 + 2 = ☐

Part 5

a. 6 − 2 = ☐

c. 3 + 2 = ☐

e. 5 − 3 = ☐

b. 2 + 6 = ☐

d. 3 − 2 = ☐

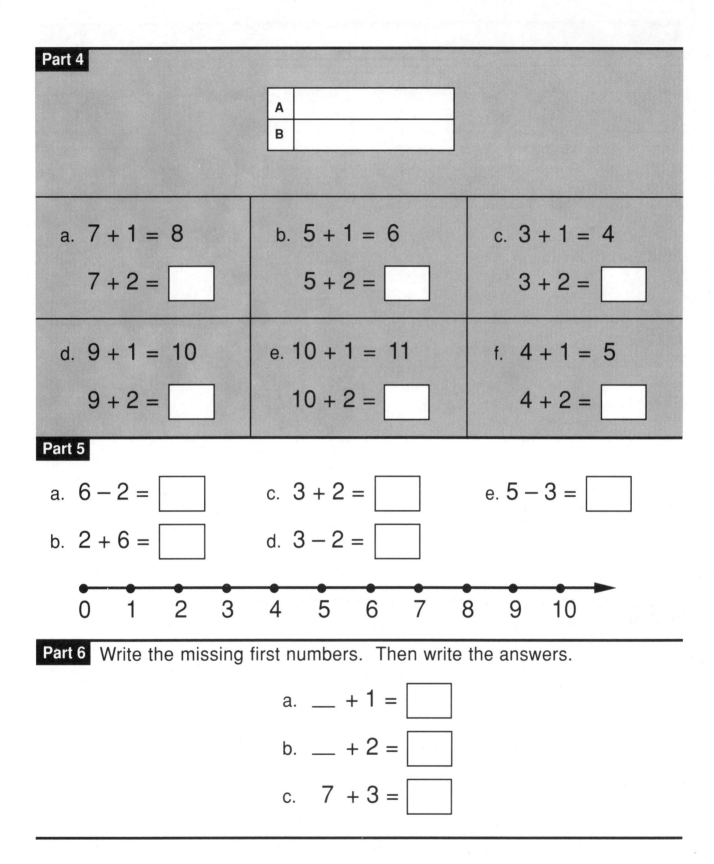

0   1   2   3   4   5   6   7   8   9   10

Part 6 Write the missing first numbers. Then write the answers.

a. __ + 1 = ☐

b. __ + 2 = ☐

c. 7 + 3 = ☐

Lesson 17

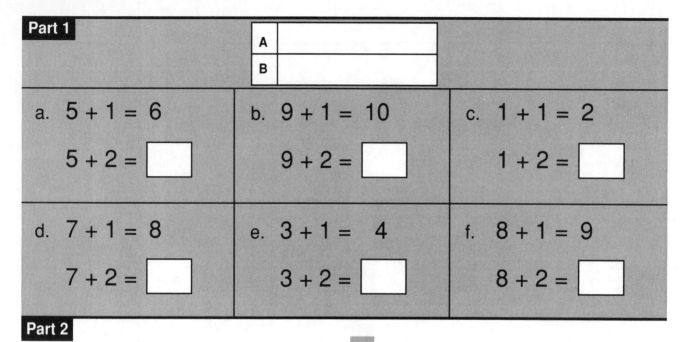

Part 1

A	
B	

a. $5 + 1 = 6$

$5 + 2 = \boxed{}$

b. $9 + 1 = 10$

$9 + 2 = \boxed{}$

c. $1 + 1 = 2$

$1 + 2 = \boxed{}$

d. $7 + 1 = 8$

$7 + 2 = \boxed{}$

e. $3 + 1 = 4$

$3 + 2 = \boxed{}$

f. $8 + 1 = 9$

$8 + 2 = \boxed{}$

Part 2

a.

b.

c.

d.

e.

Part 3

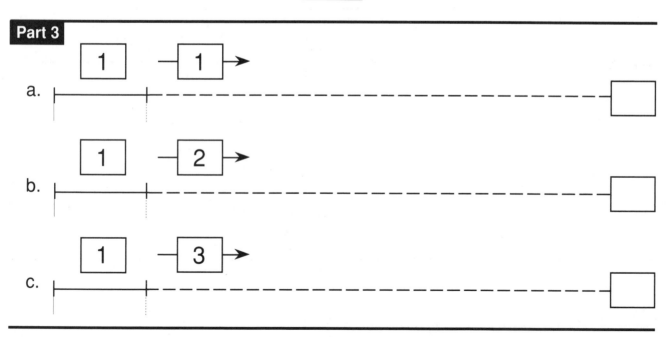

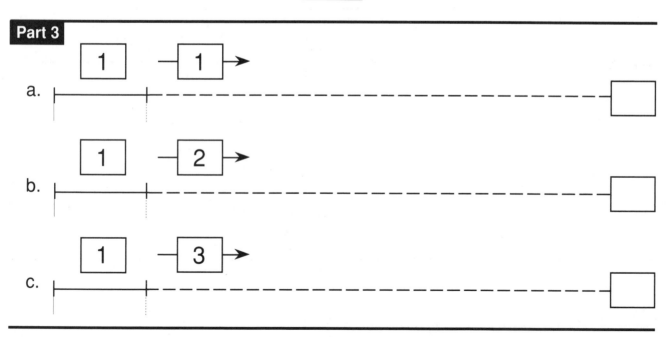

32

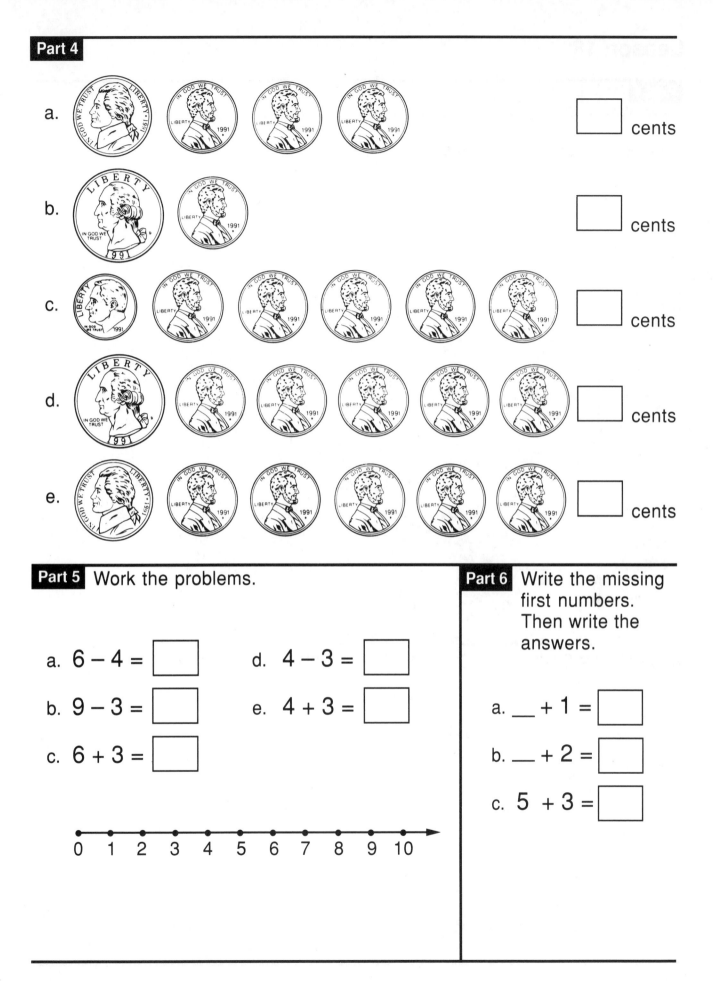

a. ☐ cents

b. ☐ cents

c. ☐ cents

d. ☐ cents

e. ☐ cents

Part 5 Work the problems.

a. $6 - 4 =$ ☐   d. $4 - 3 =$ ☐

b. $9 - 3 =$ ☐   e. $4 + 3 =$ ☐

c. $6 + 3 =$ ☐

0 1 2 3 4 5 6 7 8 9 10

Part 6 Write the missing first numbers. Then write the answers.

a. __ + 1 = ☐

b. __ + 2 = ☐

c. $5 + 3 =$ ☐

Lesson 18

a. $\underrightarrow{3 \qquad 7}$ 10

b. $\underrightarrow{2 \qquad 5}$ 7

c. $\underrightarrow{1 \qquad 9}$ 10

_____   _____   _____

_____   _____   _____

Part 2

A	
B	

a. $5 + 1 =$ ☐

$5 + 2 =$ ☐

b. $25 + 1 =$ ☐

$25 + 2 =$ ☐

c. $10 + 1 =$ ☐

$10 + 2 =$ ☐

d. $1 + 1 =$ ☐

$1 + 2 =$ ☐

e. $6 + 1 =$ ☐

$6 + 2 =$ ☐

f. $4 + 1 =$ ☐

$4 + 2 =$ ☐

Part 3 Make each line longer. Write the number at the end of each line.

a. ☐2☐   ☐1→ |————————|- - - - - - - - - - - - - - - ☐

b. ☐2☐   ☐2→ |————————|- - - - - - - - - - - - - - - ☐

c. ☐2☐   ☐3→ |————————|- - - - - - - - - - - - - - - ☐

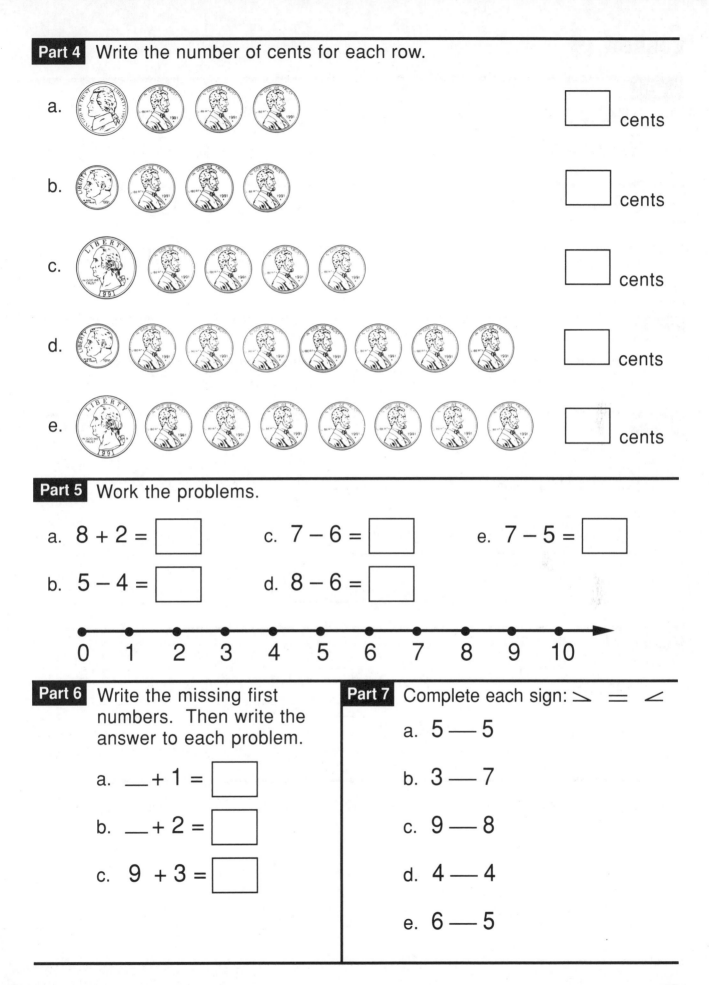

Part 4 Write the number of cents for each row.

a. ⬜ cents

b. ⬜ cents

c. ⬜ cents

d. ⬜ cents

e. ⬜ cents

Part 5 Work the problems.

a. 8 + 2 = ⬜

c. 7 − 6 = ⬜

e. 7 − 5 = ⬜

b. 5 − 4 = ⬜

d. 8 − 6 = ⬜

0 1 2 3 4 5 6 7 8 9 10

Part 6 Write the missing first numbers. Then write the answer to each problem.

a. __ + 1 = ⬜

b. __ + 2 = ⬜

c. 9 + 3 = ⬜

Part 7 Complete each sign: ＞ ＝ ＜

a. 5 — 5

b. 3 — 7

c. 9 — 8

d. 4 — 4

e. 6 — 5

35

Lesson 19

Part 1

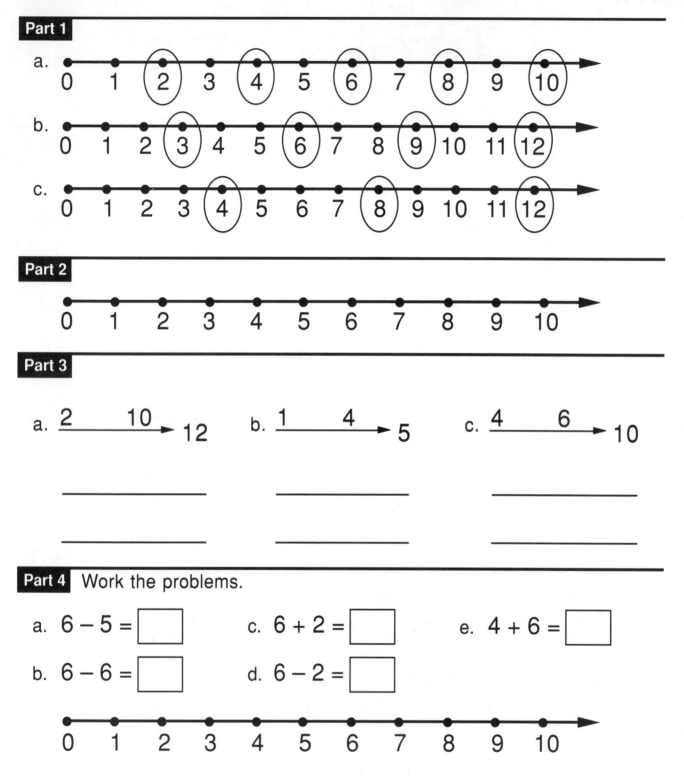

a.
0 1 (2) 3 (4) 5 (6) 7 (8) 9 (10)

b.
0 1 2 (3) 4 5 (6) 7 8 (9) 10 11 (12)

c.
0 1 2 3 (4) 5 6 7 (8) 9 10 11 (12)

Part 2

0 1 2 3 4 5 6 7 8 9 10

Part 3

a. $\dfrac{2 \qquad 10}{} \to 12$

b. $\dfrac{1 \qquad 4}{} \to 5$

c. $\dfrac{4 \qquad 6}{} \to 10$

_____   _____   _____

_____   _____   _____

Part 4 Work the problems.

a. $6 - 5 = \boxed{}$ c. $6 + 2 = \boxed{}$ e. $4 + 6 = \boxed{}$

b. $6 - 6 = \boxed{}$ d. $6 - 2 = \boxed{}$

0 1 2 3 4 5 6 7 8 9 10

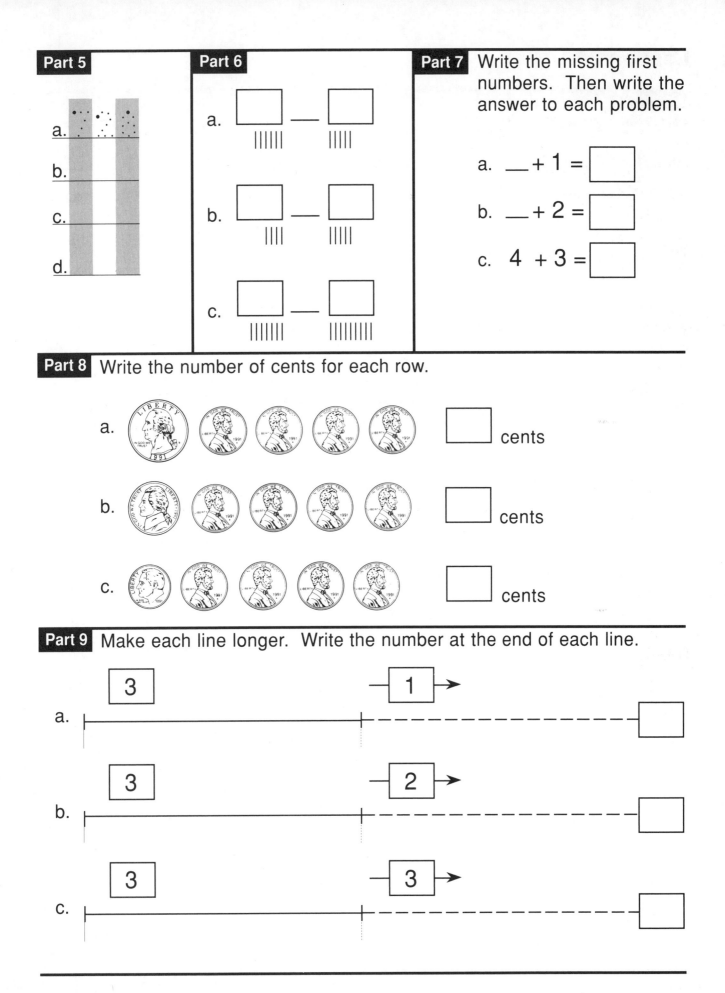

Part 5

a.

b.

c.

d.

Part 6

a. ☐ — ☐
   |||||| |||||

b. ☐ — ☐
   |||| |||||

c. ☐ — ☐
   ||||||| |||||||||

Part 7 Write the missing first numbers. Then write the answer to each problem.

a. __ + 1 = ☐

b. __ + 2 = ☐

c. 4 + 3 = ☐

Part 8 Write the number of cents for each row.

a. ☐ cents

b. ☐ cents

c. ☐ cents

Part 9 Make each line longer. Write the number at the end of each line.

a. 3 → 1 → ☐

b. 3 → 2 → ☐

c. 3 → 3 → ☐

Lesson 20

Part 1

A	
B	

a. $6 + 1 = \boxed{}$

$6 + 2 = \boxed{}$

b. $16 + 1 = \boxed{}$

$16 + 2 = \boxed{}$

c. $8 + 1 = \boxed{}$

$8 + 2 = \boxed{}$

d. $5 + 1 = \boxed{}$

$5 + 2 = \boxed{}$

e. $9 + 1 = \boxed{}$

$9 + 2 = \boxed{}$

f. $12 + 1 = \boxed{}$

$12 + 2 = \boxed{}$

Part 2

a.

b.

c.

d.

Part 3 Write the two addition facts for each number family. Start the first fact with the first small number in the family.

a. $\xrightarrow{\hspace{0.5em} 1 \qquad 7 \hspace{0.5em}} 8$

_____

_____

b. $\xrightarrow{\hspace{0.5em} 1 \qquad 3 \hspace{0.5em}} 4$

_____

_____

Part 4

a. $\boxed{}$ $\boxed{1} \rightarrow$ $\boxed{}$

b. $\boxed{}$ $\boxed{2} \rightarrow$ $\boxed{}$

c. $\boxed{}$ $\boxed{3} \rightarrow$ $\boxed{}$

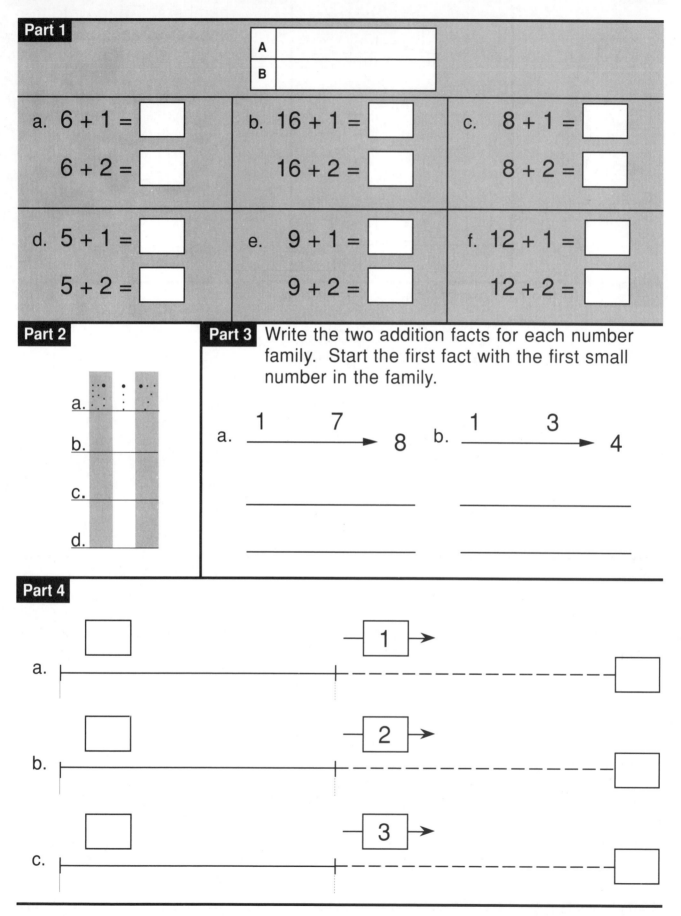

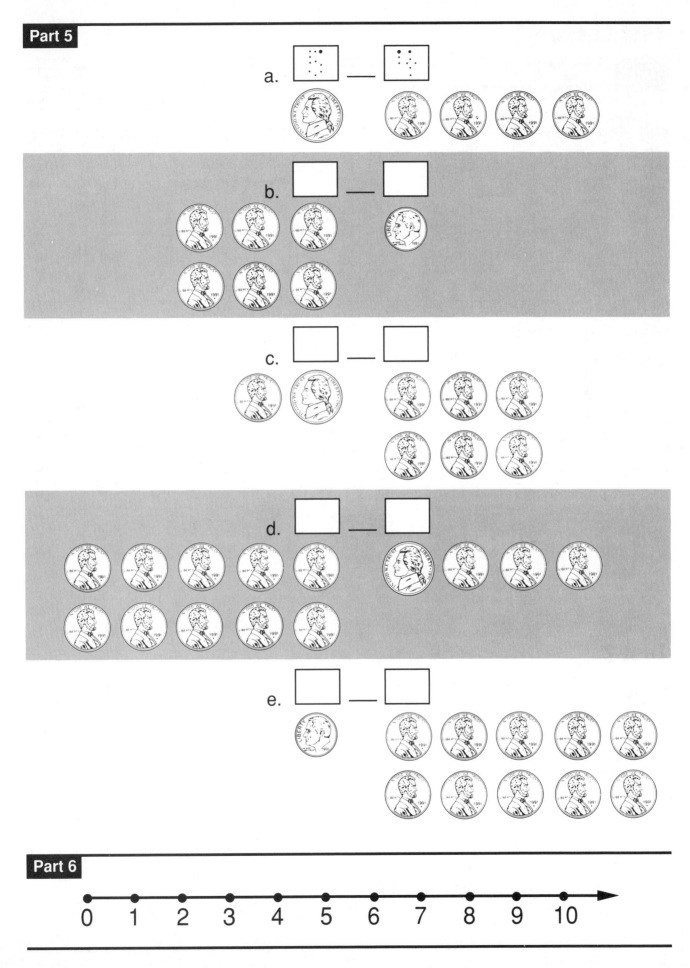

Part 5

Part 6

39

Test Lesson 2

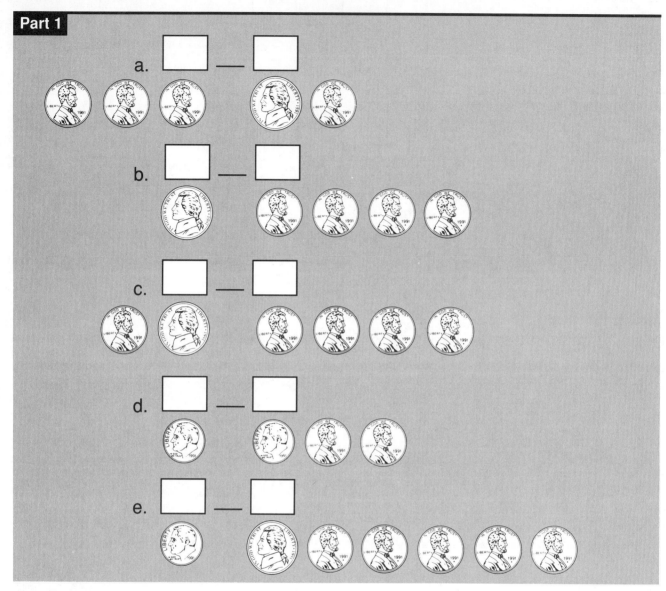

a. ☐ — ☐

b. ☐ — ☐

c. ☐ — ☐

d. ☐ — ☐

e. ☐ — ☐

Test 2

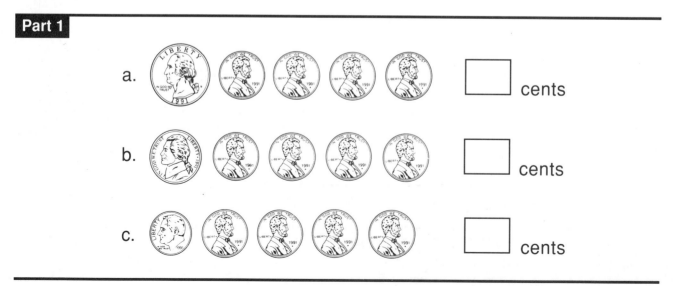

a. ☐ cents

b. ☐ cents

c. ☐ cents

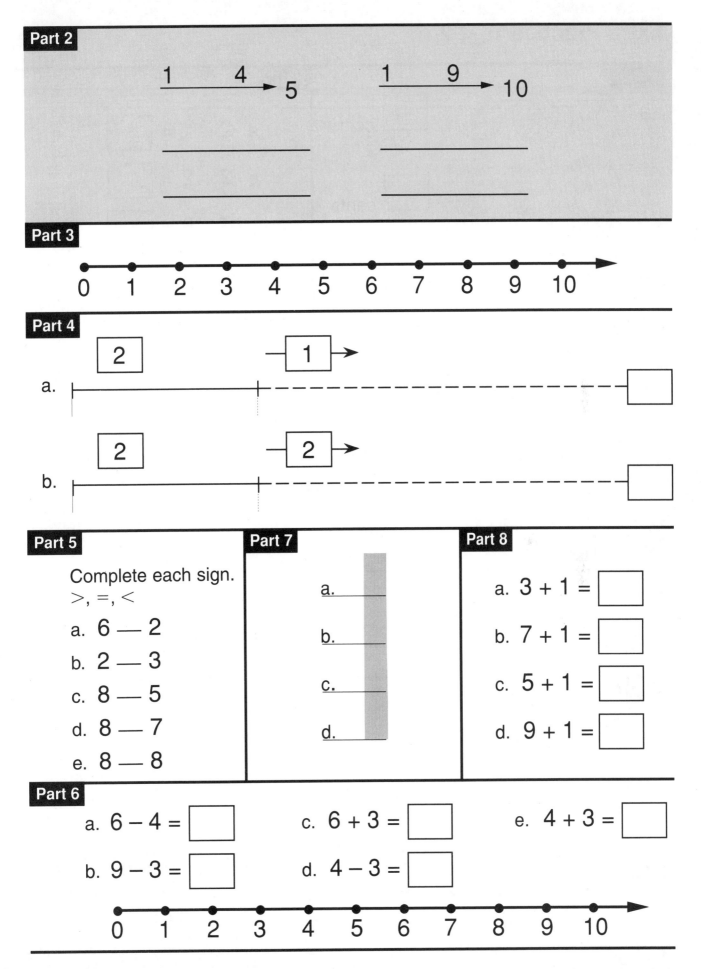

Part 2

$$1 \xrightarrow{4} 5 \qquad 1 \xrightarrow{9} 10$$

_____   _____

_____   _____

Part 3

0　1　2　3　4　5　6　7　8　9　10

Part 4

a. 2 —1→ ☐

b. 2 —2→ ☐

Part 5

Complete each sign.
>, =, <

a. 6 — 2

b. 2 — 3

c. 8 — 5

d. 8 — 7

e. 8 — 8

Part 7

a. _____

b. _____

c. _____

d. _____

Part 8

a. 3 + 1 = ☐

b. 7 + 1 = ☐

c. 5 + 1 = ☐

d. 9 + 1 = ☐

Part 6

a. 6 − 4 = ☐

b. 9 − 3 = ☐

c. 6 + 3 = ☐

d. 4 − 3 = ☐

e. 4 + 3 = ☐

0　1　2　3　4　5　6　7　8　9　10

Extra Practice/Test 2

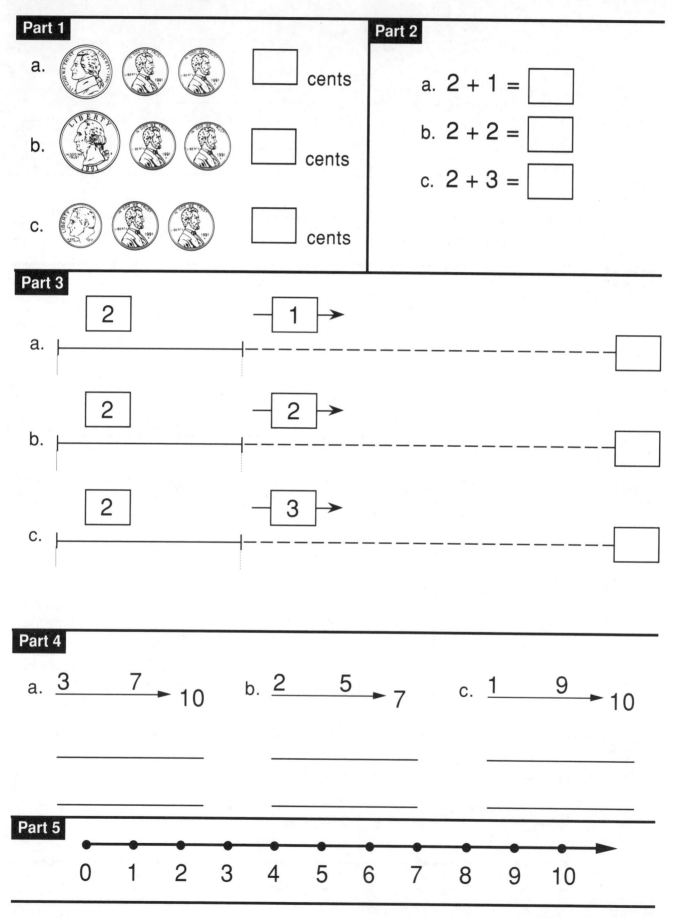

Part 1

a. [ ] cents

b. [ ] cents

c. [ ] cents

Part 2

a. 2 + 1 = [ ]

b. 2 + 2 = [ ]

c. 2 + 3 = [ ]

Part 3

a. 2 → 1 → [ ]

b. 2 → 2 → [ ]

c. 2 → 3 → [ ]

Part 4

a. 3 →7→ 10

_____

_____

b. 2 →5→ 7

_____

_____

c. 1 →9→ 10

_____

_____

Part 5

0 1 2 3 4 5 6 7 8 9 10

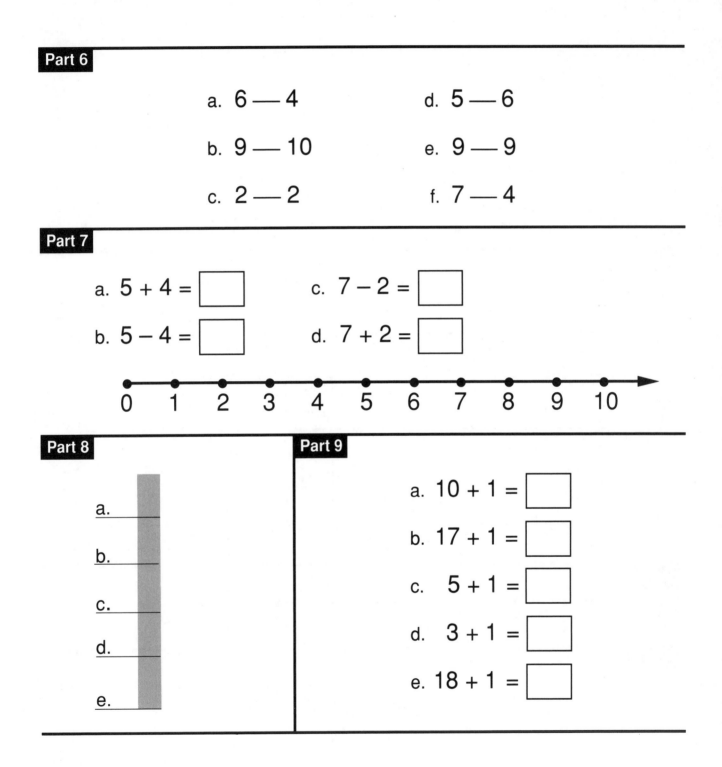

Part 6

a. 6 — 4   d. 5 — 6

b. 9 — 10   e. 9 — 9

c. 2 — 2   f. 7 — 4

Part 7

a. 5 + 4 = ☐   c. 7 − 2 = ☐

b. 5 − 4 = ☐   d. 7 + 2 = ☐

0   1   2   3   4   5   6   7   8   9   10

Part 8

a.

b.

c.

d.

e.

Part 9

a. 10 + 1 = ☐

b. 17 + 1 = ☐

c. 5 + 1 = ☐

d. 3 + 1 = ☐

e. 18 + 1 = ☐

Lesson 21

Part 1

a.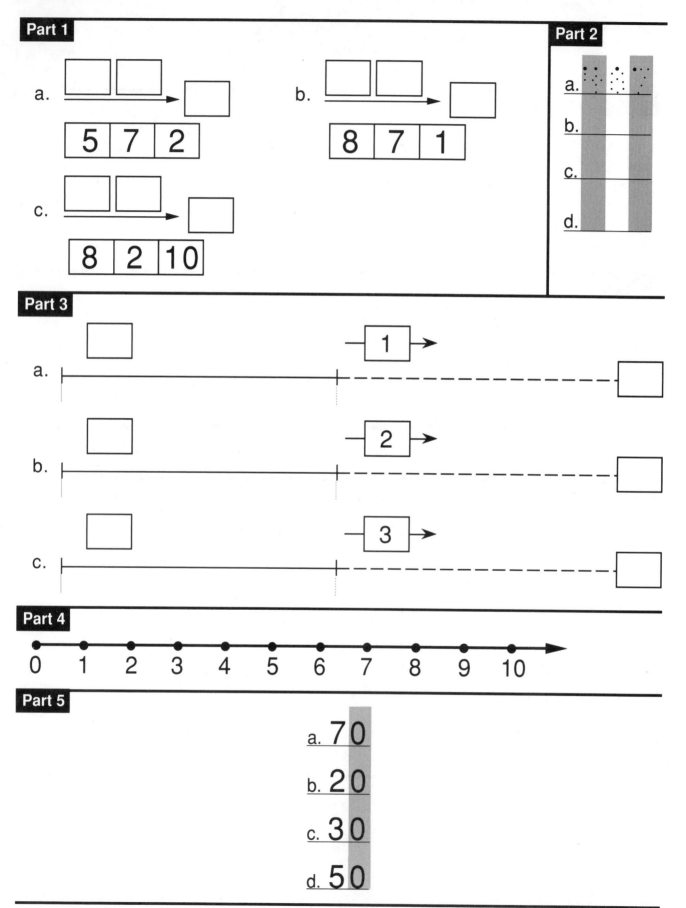

5	7	2

b.

8	7	1

c.

8	2	10

Part 2

a.

b.

c.

d.

Part 3

a. → 1 →

b. → 2 →

c. → 3 →

Part 4

0   1   2   3   4   5   6   7   8   9   10

Part 5

a. 70

b. 20

c. 30

d. 50

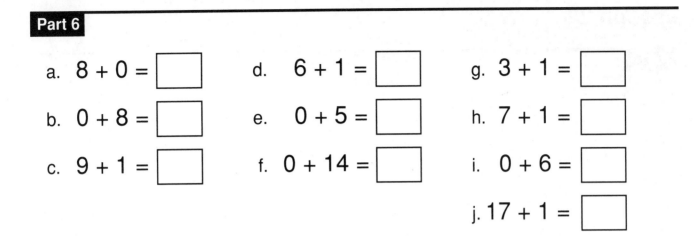

a. $8 + 0 = \boxed{}$ d. $6 + 1 = \boxed{}$ g. $3 + 1 = \boxed{}$

b. $0 + 8 = \boxed{}$ e. $0 + 5 = \boxed{}$ h. $7 + 1 = \boxed{}$

c. $9 + 1 = \boxed{}$ f. $0 + 14 = \boxed{}$ i. $0 + 6 = \boxed{}$

j. $17 + 1 = \boxed{}$

Part 7

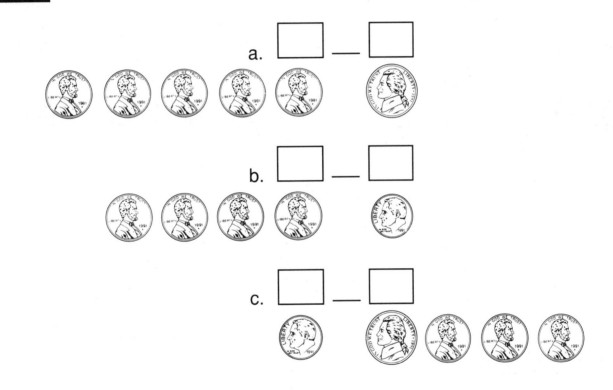

a. $\boxed{} - \boxed{}$

b. $\boxed{} - \boxed{}$

c. $\boxed{} - \boxed{}$

Part 8 Write the two addition facts for each number family. Start the first fact with the first small number in the family.

a. $\xrightarrow[\quad\quad\quad\quad]{1 \qquad 9}$ 10   b. $\xrightarrow[\quad\quad\quad\quad]{2 \qquad 6}$ 8

_____   _____

_____   _____

Lesson 22

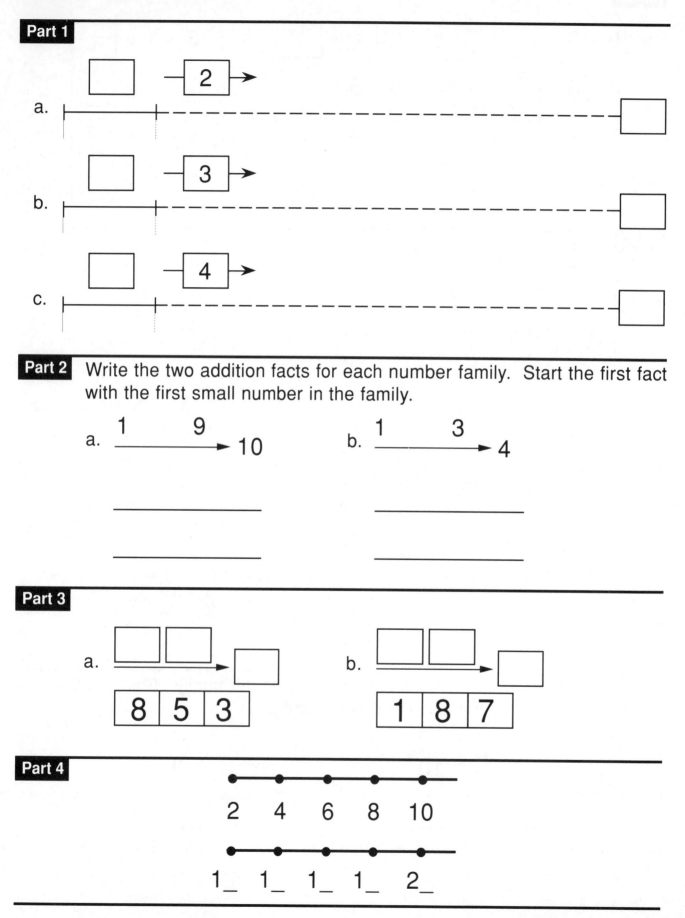

Part 2 Write the two addition facts for each number family. Start the first fact with the first small number in the family.

a. $\underset{\xrightarrow{\hspace{2cm}}}{1\qquad 9}$ 10

b. $\underset{\xrightarrow{\hspace{2cm}}}{1\qquad 3}$ 4

_____   _____

_____   _____

Part 3

a.

| 8 | 5 | 3 |

b.

| 1 | 8 | 7 |

Part 4

2   4   6   8   10

1_   1_   1_   1_   2_

Part 5

a. 83

b. 59

c. 426

Part 6

a. 37   How many digits? ☐

b. 356   How many digits? ☐

c. 3   How many digits? ☐

d. 287   How many digits? ☐

e. 40   How many digits? ☐

Part 7

a. 20

b. 50

c. 30

d. 60

Part 8

| A | |
| B | |

a. 2 + 1 = ☐
   2 + 2 = ☐

b. 7 + 1 = ☐
   7 + 2 = ☐

c. 4 + 1 = ☐
   4 + 2 = ☐

d. 5 + 1 = ☐
   5 + 2 = ☐

e. 15 + 1 = ☐
   15 + 2 = ☐

f. 10 + 1 = ☐
   10 + 2 = ☐

Part 9 Write the answers.

a. 0 + 11 = ☐

c. 7 + 0 = ☐

e. 14 + 1 = ☐

b. 2 + 1 = ☐

d. 9 + 1 = ☐

f. 0 + 4 = ☐

Lesson 23

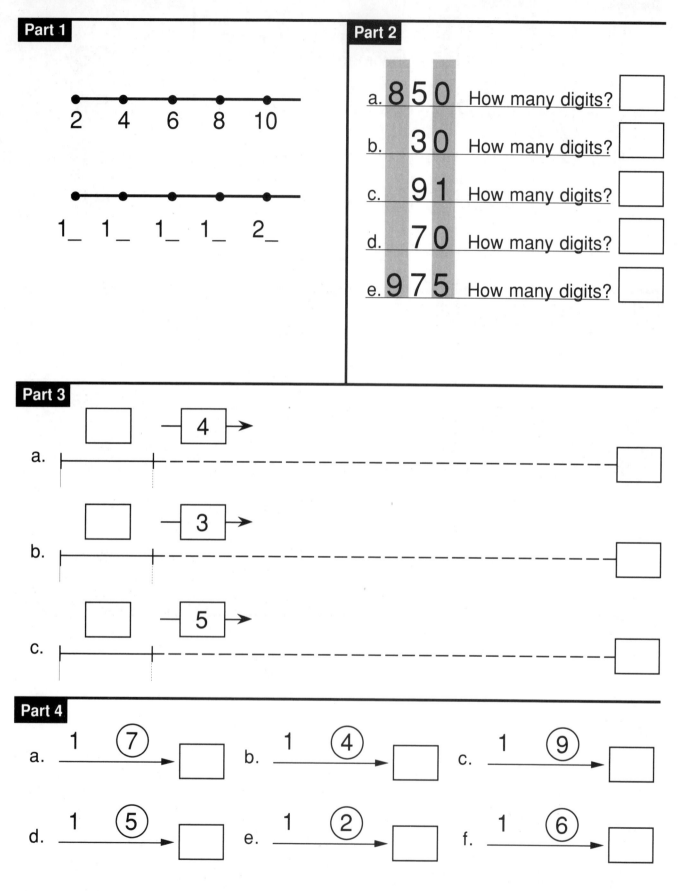

Part 1

2   4   6   8   10

1_   1_   1_   1_   2_

Part 2

a. 850   How many digits? ☐

b. 30   How many digits? ☐

c. 91   How many digits? ☐

d. 70   How many digits? ☐

e. 975   How many digits? ☐

Part 3

a. ☐ —[4]→

b. ☐ —[3]→

c. ☐ —[5]→

Part 4

a. 1 ⑦ → ☐   b. 1 ④ → ☐   c. 1 ⑨ → ☐

d. 1 ⑤ → ☐   e. 1 ② → ☐   f. 1 ⑥ → ☐

a. 8 + 1 = ☐

8 + 2 = ☐

b. 3 + 1 = ☐

3 + 2 = ☐

c. 6 + 1 = ☐

6 + 2 = ☐

Part 6 Write the two addition facts for each number family. Start the first fact with the first small number in the family.

a. 1 ──── 3 → 4

_____

_____

b. 1 ──── 8 → 9

_____

_____

Part 7

a. 12 + 0 = ☐

b. 15 + 1 = ☐

c. 20 + 0 = ☐

d. 18 + 1 = ☐

e. 7 + 0 = ☐

f. 14 + 1 = ☐

g. 0 + 11 = ☐

Part 8

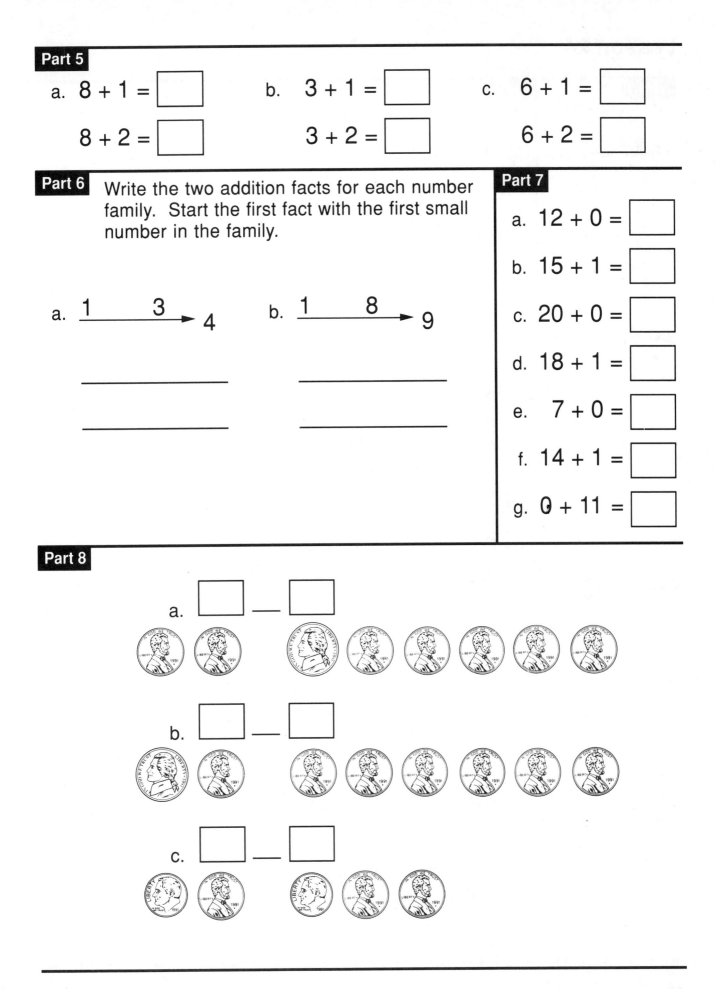

a. ☐ — ☐

b. ☐ — ☐

c. ☐ — ☐

Lesson 24

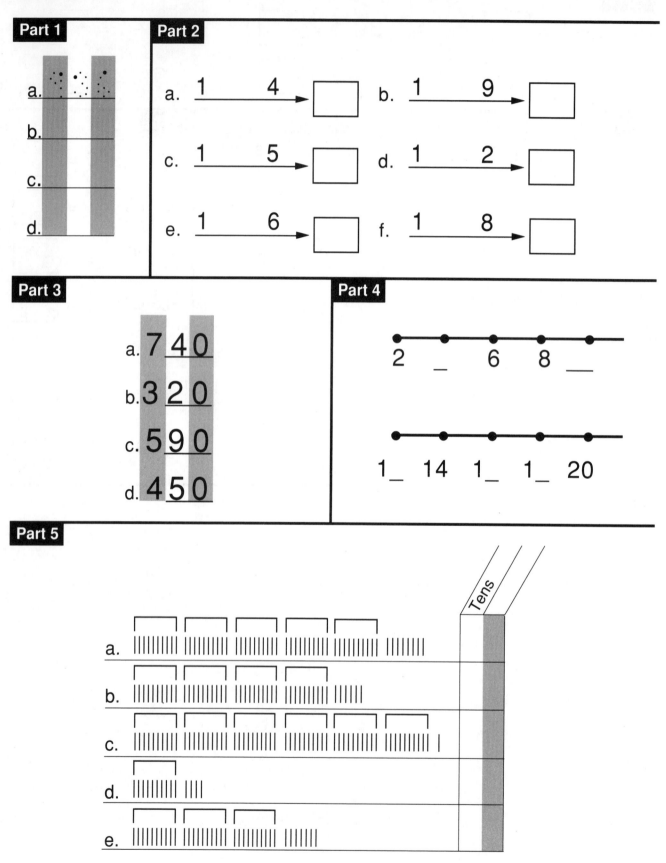

Part 1

a.

b.

c.

d.

Part 2

a. 1 ——— 4 ——→ ☐   b. 1 ——— 9 ——→ ☐

c. 1 ——— 5 ——→ ☐   d. 1 ——— 2 ——→ ☐

e. 1 ——— 6 ——→ ☐   f. 1 ——— 8 ——→ ☐

Part 3

a. 7 4 0

b. 3 2 0

c. 5 9 0

d. 4 5 0

Part 4

2 _ 6 8 _

1_ 14 1_ 1_ 20

Part 5

Tens

a.

b.

c.

d.

e.

a. $7 + 1 = \boxed{}$ b. $9 + 1 = \boxed{}$ c. $3 + 1 = \boxed{}$

   $7 + 2 = \boxed{}$ $9 + 2 = \boxed{}$ $3 + 2 = \boxed{}$

Part 7

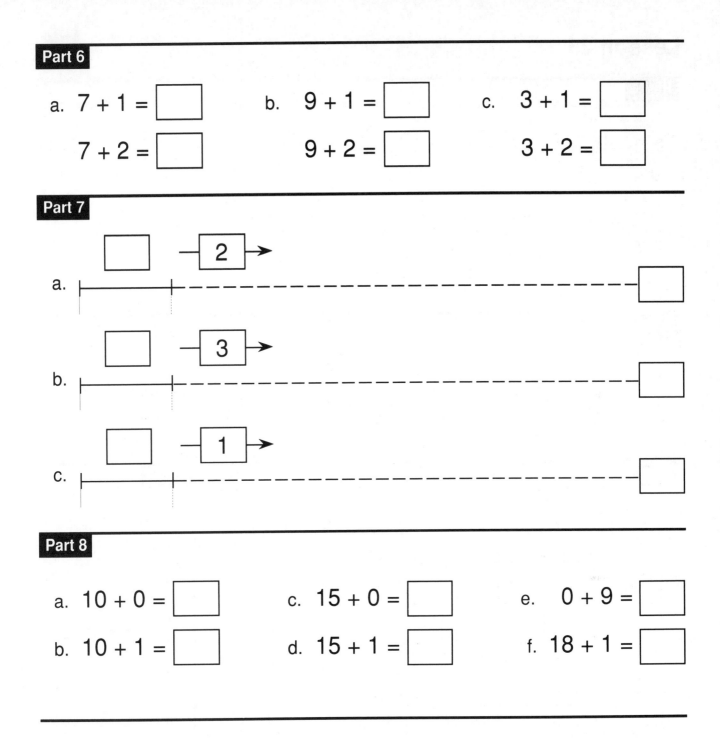

Part 8

a. $10 + 0 = \boxed{}$ c. $15 + 0 = \boxed{}$ e. $0 + 9 = \boxed{}$

b. $10 + 1 = \boxed{}$ d. $15 + 1 = \boxed{}$ f. $18 + 1 = \boxed{}$

Lesson 25

Part 1

a. 1 ⟶ 3 ▢

b. 1 ⟶ 10 ▢

c. 1 ⟶ 5 ▢

d. 1 ⟶ 7 ▢

e. 1 ⟶ 4 ▢

f. 1 ⟶ 2 ▢

Part 2

a. 1 + 5 = ▢

c. 1 + 9 = ▢

e. 1 + 7 = ▢

b. 1 + 3 = ▢

d. 1 + 4 = ▢

f. 1 + 2 = ▢

Part 3

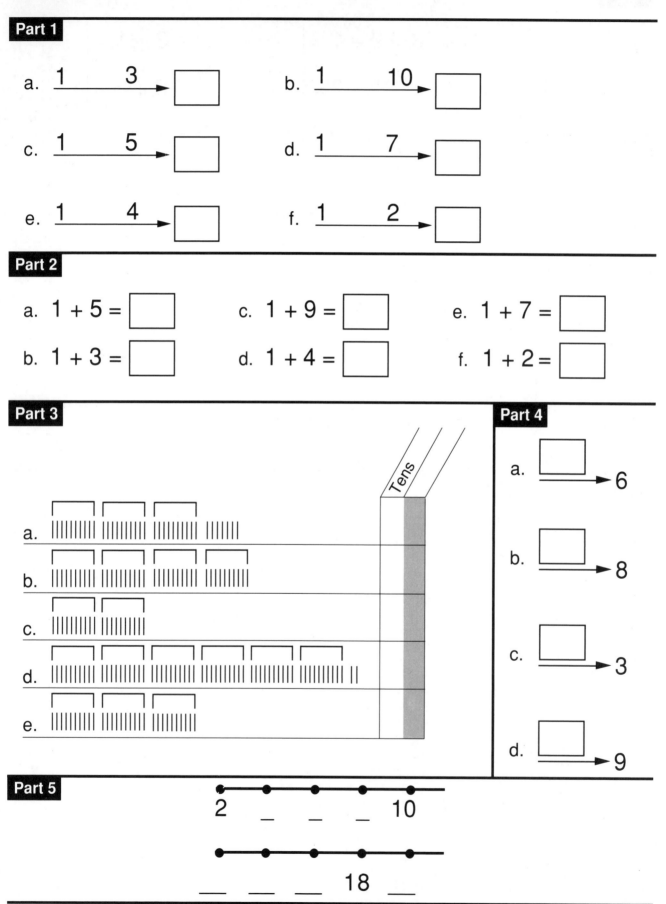

Tens

a.

b.

c.

d.

e.

Part 4

a. ▢ ⟶ 6

b. ▢ ⟶ 8

c. ▢ ⟶ 3

d. ▢ ⟶ 9

Part 5

2 __ __ __ 10

__ __ __ 18 __

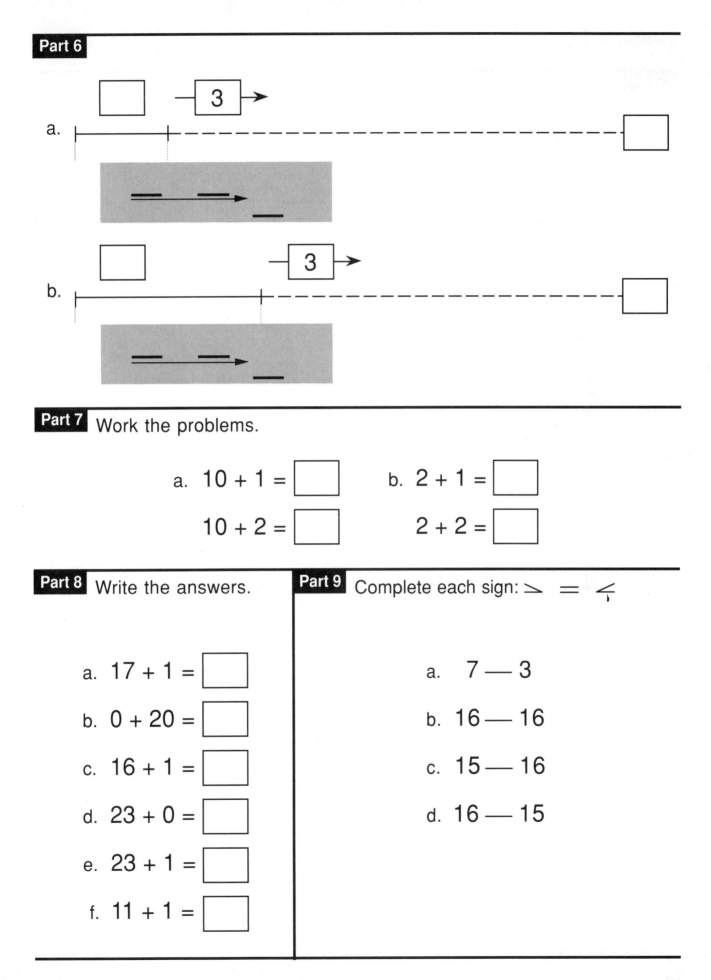

Part 7 Work the problems.

a. $10 + 1 = \boxed{}$

$10 + 2 = \boxed{}$

b. $2 + 1 = \boxed{}$

$2 + 2 = \boxed{}$

Part 8 Write the answers.

a. $17 + 1 = \boxed{}$

b. $0 + 20 = \boxed{}$

c. $16 + 1 = \boxed{}$

d. $23 + 0 = \boxed{}$

e. $23 + 1 = \boxed{}$

f. $11 + 1 = \boxed{}$

Part 9 Complete each sign: $>$ $=$ $<$

a. $7 \;\text{---}\; 3$

b. $16 \;\text{---}\; 16$

c. $15 \;\text{---}\; 16$

d. $16 \;\text{---}\; 15$

Lesson 26

Part 1

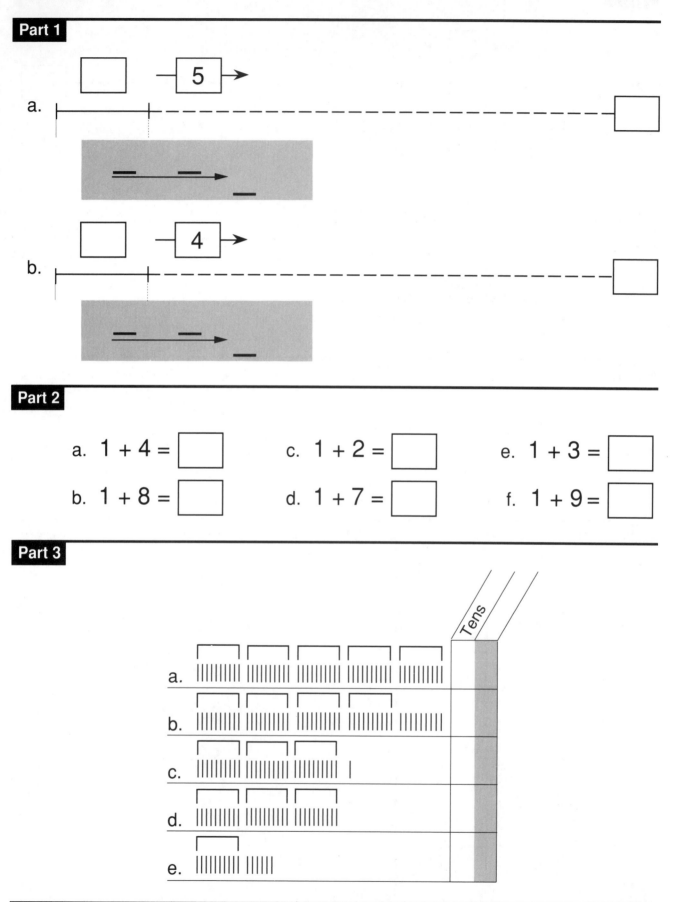

Part 2

a. $1 + 4 = \boxed{}$ c. $1 + 2 = \boxed{}$ e. $1 + 3 = \boxed{}$

b. $1 + 8 = \boxed{}$ d. $1 + 7 = \boxed{}$ f. $1 + 9 = \boxed{}$

Part 3

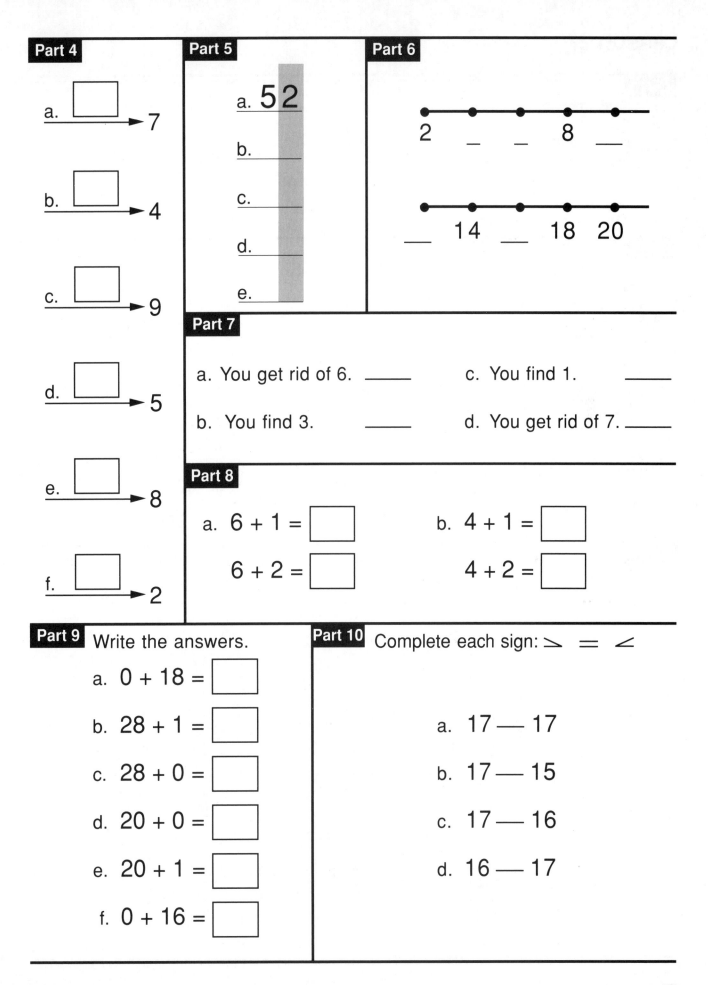

Part 4

a. [ ] → 7

b. [ ] → 4

c. [ ] → 9

d. [ ] → 5

e. [ ] → 8

f. [ ] → 2

Part 5

a. 5 2

b. _____

c. _____

d. _____

e. _____

Part 6

2 _ _ 8 _

_ 14 _ 18 20

Part 7

a. You get rid of 6. _____

b. You find 3. _____

c. You find 1. _____

d. You get rid of 7. _____

Part 8

a. 6 + 1 = [ ]

6 + 2 = [ ]

b. 4 + 1 = [ ]

4 + 2 = [ ]

Part 9 Write the answers.

a. 0 + 18 = [ ]

b. 28 + 1 = [ ]

c. 28 + 0 = [ ]

d. 20 + 0 = [ ]

e. 20 + 1 = [ ]

f. 0 + 16 = [ ]

Part 10 Complete each sign: > = <

a. 17 — 17

b. 17 — 15

c. 17 — 16

d. 16 — 17

Lesson 27

Part 1

a. 1
    + 5

b. 1
    + 7

c. 1
    + 4

d. 1
    + 6

e. 1
    + 3

Part 2

a.

b.

c.

d.

e.

Part 3

a. □ → 9

b. □ → 3

c. □ → 7

d. □ → 2

e. □ → 5

f. □ → 10

Part 4

Tens

a. ||||

b. |||

c. |||||||| |||||||| ||||||||

d. |||||

e. |||||||| |||||||| |||||||| |||||||| ||||||||

f. |||||||| |||||||| ||||||

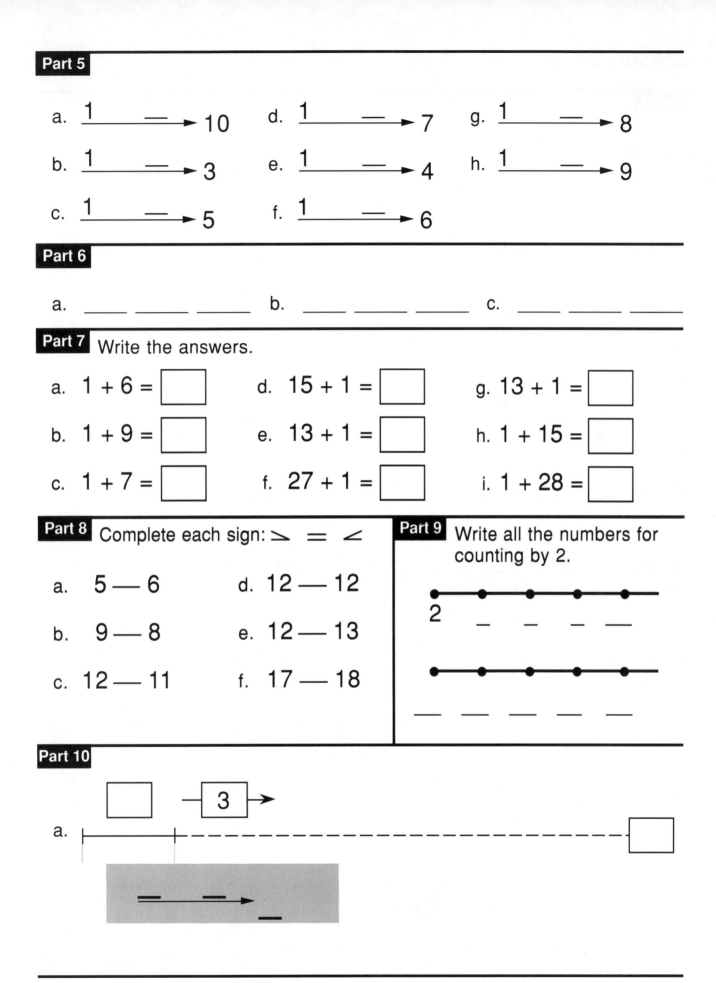

Part 5

a. 1 ———→ 10

b. 1 ———→ 3

c. 1 ———→ 5

d. 1 ———→ 7

e. 1 ———→ 4

f. 1 ———→ 6

g. 1 ———→ 8

h. 1 ———→ 9

Part 6

a. ____ ____ ____ ____

b. ____ ____ ____ ____

c. ____ ____ ____ ____

Part 7 Write the answers.

a. 1 + 6 = ☐

b. 1 + 9 = ☐

c. 1 + 7 = ☐

d. 15 + 1 = ☐

e. 13 + 1 = ☐

f. 27 + 1 = ☐

g. 13 + 1 = ☐

h. 1 + 15 = ☐

i. 1 + 28 = ☐

Part 8 Complete each sign: > = <

a. 5 — 6

b. 9 — 8

c. 12 — 11

d. 12 — 12

e. 12 — 13

f. 17 — 18

Part 9 Write all the numbers for counting by 2.

2 ____ ____ ____ ____

____ ____ ____ ____

Part 10

a.

☐ —[3]→

—— —→
——

Lesson 28

Part 1

a. $\dfrac{1}{} \xrightarrow{\quad-\quad} 4$

b. $\dfrac{1}{} \xrightarrow{\quad-\quad} 8$

c. $\dfrac{1}{} \xrightarrow{\quad-\quad} 3$

d. $\dfrac{1}{} \xrightarrow{\quad-\quad} 7$

e. $\dfrac{1}{} \xrightarrow{\quad-\quad} 5$

f. $\dfrac{1}{} \xrightarrow{\quad-\quad} 9$

Part 2

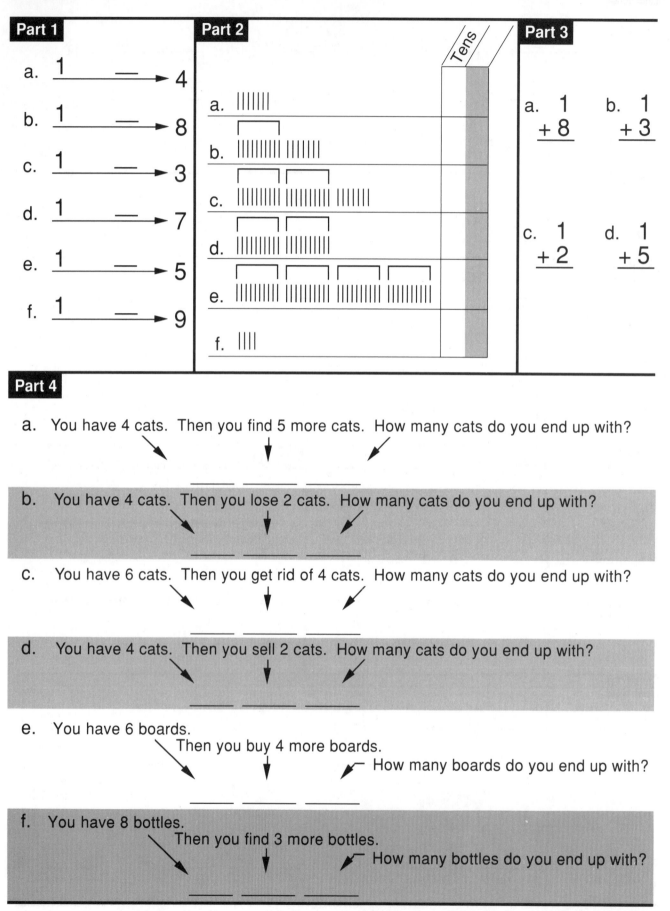

a. |||||||

b. ||||||||| |||||||

c. ||||||||| ||||||||| |||||||

d. ||||||||| |||||||||

e. ||||||||| ||||||||| ||||||||| |||||||||

f. ||||

Part 3

a. $\begin{array}{r} 1 \\ +\,8 \\ \hline \end{array}$ b. $\begin{array}{r} 1 \\ +\,3 \\ \hline \end{array}$

c. $\begin{array}{r} 1 \\ +\,2 \\ \hline \end{array}$ d. $\begin{array}{r} 1 \\ +\,5 \\ \hline \end{array}$

Part 4

a. You have 4 cats. Then you find 5 more cats. How many cats do you end up with?

____ ____ ____

b. You have 4 cats. Then you lose 2 cats. How many cats do you end up with?

____ ____ ____

c. You have 6 cats. Then you get rid of 4 cats. How many cats do you end up with?

____ ____ ____

d. You have 4 cats. Then you sell 2 cats. How many cats do you end up with?

____ ____ ____

e. You have 6 boards. Then you buy 4 more boards. How many boards do you end up with?

____ ____ ____

f. You have 8 bottles. Then you find 3 more bottles. How many bottles do you end up with?

____ ____ ____

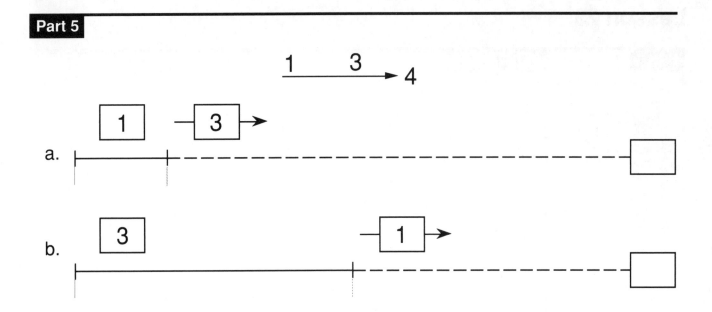

a.

b.

a. 3 ■ 5 ■ 2   ■   ■

b. 7 ■ 1 ■ 6   ■   ■

c. 8 ■ 2 ■ 6   ■   ■

d. 1 ■ 7 ■ 6   ■   ■

e. 7 ■ 5 ■ 2   ■   ■

Write all the numbers for counting by 2.

— — — — —

— — — — —

Write the answers.

a. 1 + 6 = ☐

b. 1 + 16 = ☐

c. 1 + 18 = ☐

d. 0 + 20 = ☐

e. 1 + 20 = ☐

f. 1 + 27 = ☐

g. 17 + 0 = ☐

Lesson 29

Part 1

a. _____

b. _____

c. _____

d. _____

Part 2

a. 1 ————7——→ _

b. 1 ————__——→ 9

c. 1 ————6——→ _

d. 1 ————__——→ 8

e. 1 ————5——→ _

f. 1 ————__——→ 4

g. 1 ————__——→ 6

h. 1 ————__——→ 5

i. 1 ————4——→ _

j. 1 ————8——→ _

Part 3

a. Tim has 6 dimes. He gets 3 more dimes. How many dimes does he end up with?

_____ _____ _____

b. You have 3 bikes. You sell 2 bikes. How many bikes do you end up with?

_____ _____ _____

c. Rita has 8 shoes. She loses 2 shoes. How many shoes does she end up with?

_____ _____ _____

d. Tim has 18 dollars. He spends 6 dollars. How many dollars does he end up with?

_____ _____ _____

e. You walk 1 mile. Then you walk 2 more miles. How many miles do you end up walking?

_____ _____ _____

Part 4

Tens |

a. 5 groups of ten + 6 leftovers

b. 7 groups of ten + no leftovers

c. No groups of ten, but 6 leftovers

d. 6 groups of ten + 3 leftovers

e. 9 groups of ten + no leftovers

f. No groups of ten, but 2 leftovers

g. 5 groups of ten + 4 leftovers

Part 5

a. 3   3
   + 1   + 2

b. 6   6
   + 1   + 2

c. 5   5
   + 1   + 2

d. 7   7
   + 1   + 2

Part 6

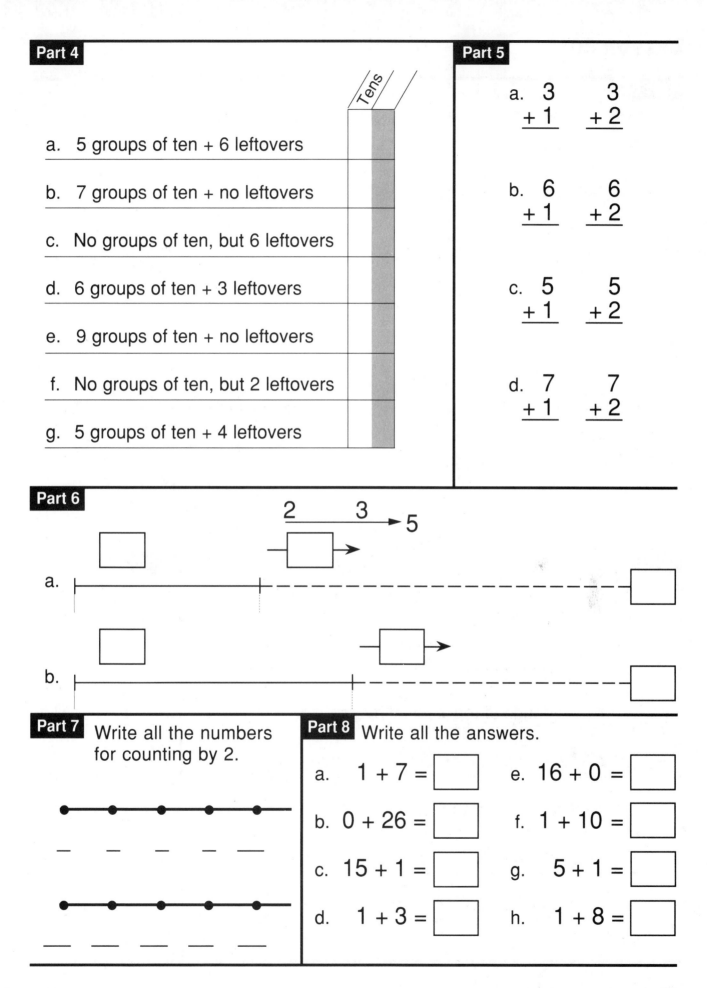

Part 7 Write all the numbers for counting by 2.

Part 8 Write all the answers.

a. 1 + 7 = ☐   e. 16 + 0 = ☐

b. 0 + 26 = ☐   f. 1 + 10 = ☐

c. 15 + 1 = ☐   g. 5 + 1 = ☐

d. 1 + 3 = ☐   h. 1 + 8 = ☐

61

Lesson 30

a. She had 4 dogs. Then she found 1 more dog. How many dogs did she end up with?

_____ — _____ _____

b. She had 8 dogs. She sold 5 dogs. How many dogs did she end up with?

_____ — _____ _____

c. Kay had 3 brooms. She got rid of 1 broom. How many brooms did she end up with?

_____ — _____ _____

d. Sandra had 6 coats.
            Then she gave away 4 coats.
                              How many coats did she end up with?

_____ — _____ _____

e. Don had 4 kites. He made 6 more kites. How many kites did he end up with?

_____ — _____ _____

Part 2

	Tens	
a. 4 groups of ten + 9 leftovers		
b. 7 groups of ten + no leftovers		
c. No groups of ten, but 5 leftovers		
d. No groups of ten, but 4 leftovers		
e. 1 group of ten + 7 leftovers		
f. 1 group of ten + no leftovers		

Part 3

a. $\begin{array}{r} 6 \\ +1 \\ \hline \end{array}$ $\begin{array}{r} 6 \\ +2 \\ \hline \end{array}$

b. $\begin{array}{r} 2 \\ +1 \\ \hline \end{array}$ $\begin{array}{r} 2 \\ +2 \\ \hline \end{array}$

c. $\begin{array}{r} 7 \\ +1 \\ \hline \end{array}$ $\begin{array}{r} 7 \\ +2 \\ \hline \end{array}$

d. $\begin{array}{r} 4 \\ +1 \\ \hline \end{array}$ $\begin{array}{r} 4 \\ +2 \\ \hline \end{array}$

Part 4

$$1 \xrightarrow{\quad 4 \quad} 5$$

a.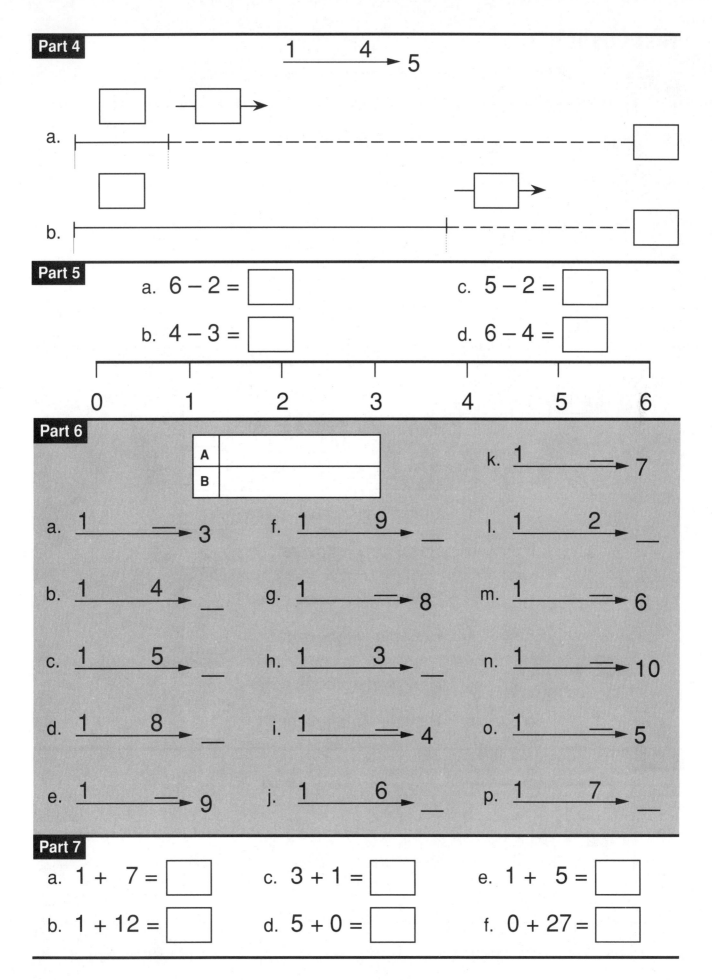

b.

Part 5

a. $6 - 2 = \boxed{}$ c. $5 - 2 = \boxed{}$

b. $4 - 3 = \boxed{}$ d. $6 - 4 = \boxed{}$

0   1   2   3   4   5   6

Part 6

| A | |
| B | |

k. $1 \xrightarrow{\quad\quad} 7$

a. $1 \xrightarrow{\quad\quad} 3$ f. $1 \xrightarrow{\quad 9 \quad} \underline{}$ l. $1 \xrightarrow{\quad 2 \quad} \underline{}$

b. $1 \xrightarrow{\quad 4 \quad} \underline{}$ g. $1 \xrightarrow{\quad\quad} 8$ m. $1 \xrightarrow{\quad\quad} 6$

c. $1 \xrightarrow{\quad 5 \quad} \underline{}$ h. $1 \xrightarrow{\quad 3 \quad} \underline{}$ n. $1 \xrightarrow{\quad\quad} 10$

d. $1 \xrightarrow{\quad 8 \quad} \underline{}$ i. $1 \xrightarrow{\quad\quad} 4$ o. $1 \xrightarrow{\quad\quad} 5$

e. $1 \xrightarrow{\quad\quad} 9$ j. $1 \xrightarrow{\quad 6 \quad} \underline{}$ p. $1 \xrightarrow{\quad 7 \quad} \underline{}$

Part 7

a. $1 + 7 = \boxed{}$ c. $3 + 1 = \boxed{}$ e. $1 + 5 = \boxed{}$

b. $1 + 12 = \boxed{}$ d. $5 + 0 = \boxed{}$ f. $0 + 27 = \boxed{}$

Test Lesson 3

Part 1

a. No groups of ten, but 8 leftovers

b. 3 groups of ten + 8 leftovers

c. No groups of ten, but 1 leftover

d. 4 groups of ten + no leftovers

e. 4 groups of ten + 1 leftover

Tens

Part 2

Tens

a. 5 2
How many groups of ten?
How many leftovers?

b. 7 0
How many groups of ten?
How many leftovers?

c. 7
How many groups of ten?
How many leftovers?

d. 1 7
How many groups of ten?
How many leftovers?

Part 3

1   3   4

a.

b.

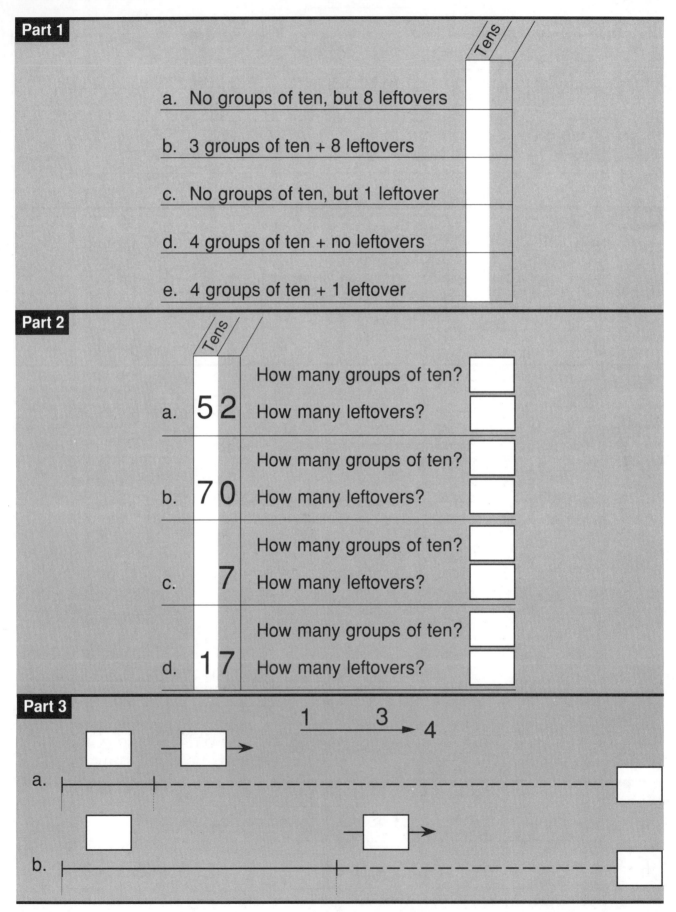

Test 3

Part 1 Write the missing number in each number family.

a. $\dfrac{1}{} \xrightarrow{} 6$

b. $\dfrac{1}{} \xrightarrow{} 9$

c. $\dfrac{1}{} \xrightarrow{} 4$

d. $\dfrac{1 \qquad 2}{} \xrightarrow{}$ ___

e. $\dfrac{1 \qquad 5}{} \xrightarrow{}$ ___

f. $\dfrac{1 \qquad 8}{} \xrightarrow{}$ ___

g. $\dfrac{1 \qquad 7}{} \xrightarrow{}$ ___

h. $\dfrac{1 \qquad 9}{} \xrightarrow{}$ ___

Part 2 Write the answer to each problem.

a. 6 + 1 = ☐   d. 1 + 5 = ☐   g. 1 + 6 = ☐

b. 1 + 9 = ☐   e. 1 + 3 = ☐   h. 1 + 8 = ☐

c. 4 + 1 = ☐   f. 2 + 1 = ☐   i. 5 + 1 = ☐

                                        j. 1 + 7 = ☐

Part 3 Write the symbols for each word problem.

a. Tim has 6 dimes. He gets 3 more dimes. How many dimes does he end up with?

_____ _____ _____

b. You have 3 bikes. You sell 2 bikes. How many bikes do you end up with?

_____ _____ _____

c. You walk 1 mile.
          Then you walk 2 more miles.
                              How many miles do you end up walking?

_____ _____ _____

Part 4 Write the answers for each pair of problems.

a. $\begin{array}{r} 6 \\ +1 \\ \hline \end{array}$ $\begin{array}{r} 6 \\ +2 \\ \hline \end{array}$ b. $\begin{array}{r} 2 \\ +1 \\ \hline \end{array}$ $\begin{array}{r} 2 \\ +2 \\ \hline \end{array}$ c. $\begin{array}{r} 4 \\ +1 \\ \hline \end{array}$ $\begin{array}{r} 4 \\ +2 \\ \hline \end{array}$

Part 5 Write all the numbers for counting by 2.

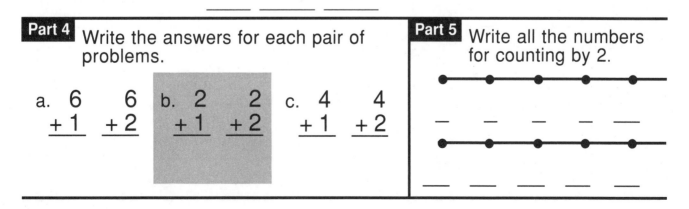

Extra Practice/Test 3

a. 1   7   → _

b. 1   —→ 9

c. 1   6   → _

d. 1   —→ 8

e. 1   5   → _

f. 1   —→ 4

g. 1   —→ 6

h. 1   —→ 5

i. 1   4   → _

j. 1   8   → _

Part 2 Write the answers.

a. 1 + 6 = ☐

b. 1 + 9 = ☐

c. 1 + 7 = ☐

d. 15 + 1 = ☐

e. 13 + 1 = ☐

f. 27 + 1 = ☐

g. 13 + 1 = ☐

h. 1 + 15 = ☐

i. 1 + 28 = ☐

Part 3

a. ___ ___ ___   b. ___ ___ ___   c. ___ ___ ___

Part 4

a. 2 + 1 = ☐

   2 + 2 = ☐

b. 7 + 1 = ☐

   7 + 2 = ☐

c. 4 + 1 = ☐

   4 + 2 = ☐

d. 5 + 1 = ☐

   5 + 2 = ☐

e. 15 + 1 = ☐

   15 + 2 = ☐

f. 10 + 1 = ☐

   10 + 2 = ☐

Lesson 31

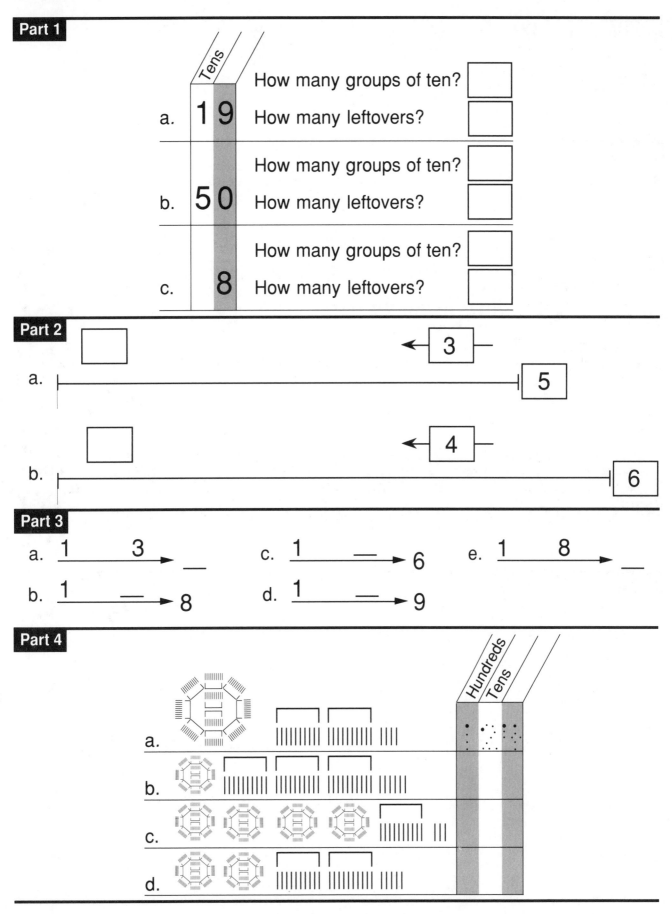

Part 1

Tens

a. 1 9
How many groups of ten?
How many leftovers?

b. 5 0
How many groups of ten?
How many leftovers?

c. 8
How many groups of ten?
How many leftovers?

Part 2

a. ☐ ← 3 ┤ ├ 5

b. ☐ ← 4 ┤ ├ 6

Part 3

a. 1 ──3──→ __   c. 1 ──—──→ 6   e. 1 ──8──→ __

b. 1 ──—──→ 8   d. 1 ──—──→ 9

Part 4

Hundreds Tens

a.

b.

c.

d.

Part 5

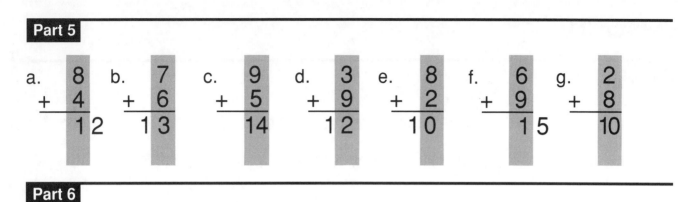

a.
```
  8
+ 4
 12
```
b.
```
  7
+ 6
 13
```
c.
```
  9
+ 5
 14
```
d.
```
  3
+ 9
 12
```
e.
```
  8
+ 2
 10
```
f.
```
  6
+ 9
 15
```
g.
```
  2
+ 8
 10
```

Part 6

a. You have 9 marbles. Then you lose 8 marbles. How many marbles do you end up with?

_____ _____ _____

b. You have 6 dogs. Then you buy 1 more dog. How many dogs do you end up with?

_____ _____ _____

c. You have 1 box. Then you make 8 more boxes. How many boxes do you end up with?

_____ _____ _____

d. You have 4 pens. Then you give away 3 pens. How many pens do you end up with?

_____ _____ _____

Part 7

a.
```
  8    8
+ 1  + 2
```
b.
```
  4    4
+ 1  + 2
```

c.
```
  7    7
+ 1  + 2
```
d.
```
  5    5
+ 1  + 2
```

Lesson 32

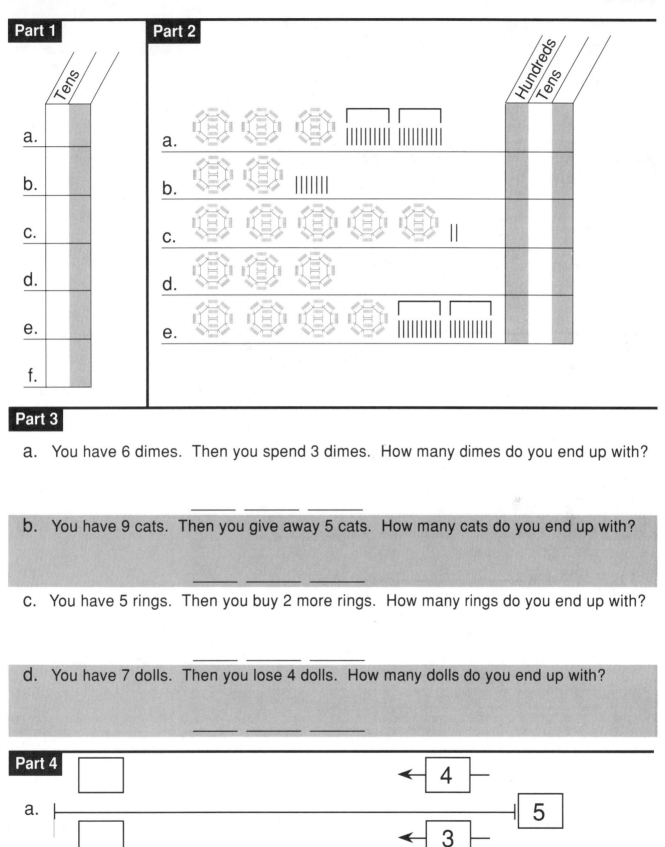

Part 1

Tens

a.

b.

c.

d.

e.

f.

Part 2

Hundreds Tens

a.

b.

c.

d.

e.

Part 3

a. You have 6 dimes. Then you spend 3 dimes. How many dimes do you end up with?

_____ _____ _____

b. You have 9 cats. Then you give away 5 cats. How many cats do you end up with?

_____ _____ _____

c. You have 5 rings. Then you buy 2 more rings. How many rings do you end up with?

_____ _____ _____

d. You have 7 dolls. Then you lose 4 dolls. How many dolls do you end up with?

_____ _____ _____

Part 4

a. ← 4 ⊢   5

b. ← 3 ⊢   5

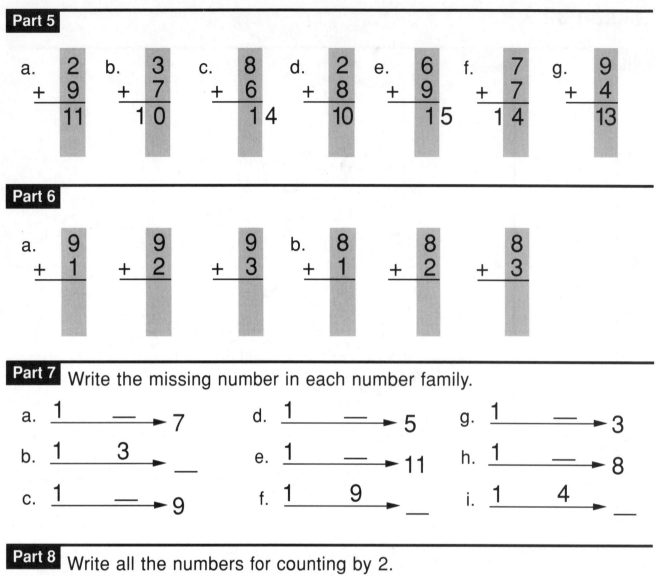

a.
```
   2
+  9
  11
```

b.
```
   3
+  7
  10
```

c.
```
   8
+  6
  14
```

d.
```
   2
+  8
  10
```

e.
```
   6
+  9
  15
```

f.
```
   7
+  7
  14
```

g.
```
   9
+  4
  13
```

Part 6

a.
```
   9
+  1
```

```
   9
+  2
```

```
   9
+  3
```

b.
```
   8
+  1
```

```
   8
+  2
```

```
   8
+  3
```

Part 7 Write the missing number in each number family.

a. 1 —→ 7

b. 1   3 —→ __

c. 1 —→ 9

d. 1 —→ 5

e. 1 —→ 11

f. 1   9 —→ __

g. 1 —→ 3

h. 1 —→ 8

i. 1   4 —→ __

Part 8 Write all the numbers for counting by 2.

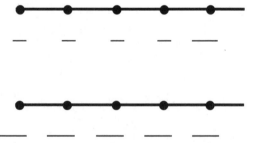

__ __ __ __ __

__ __ __ __ __

Lesson 33

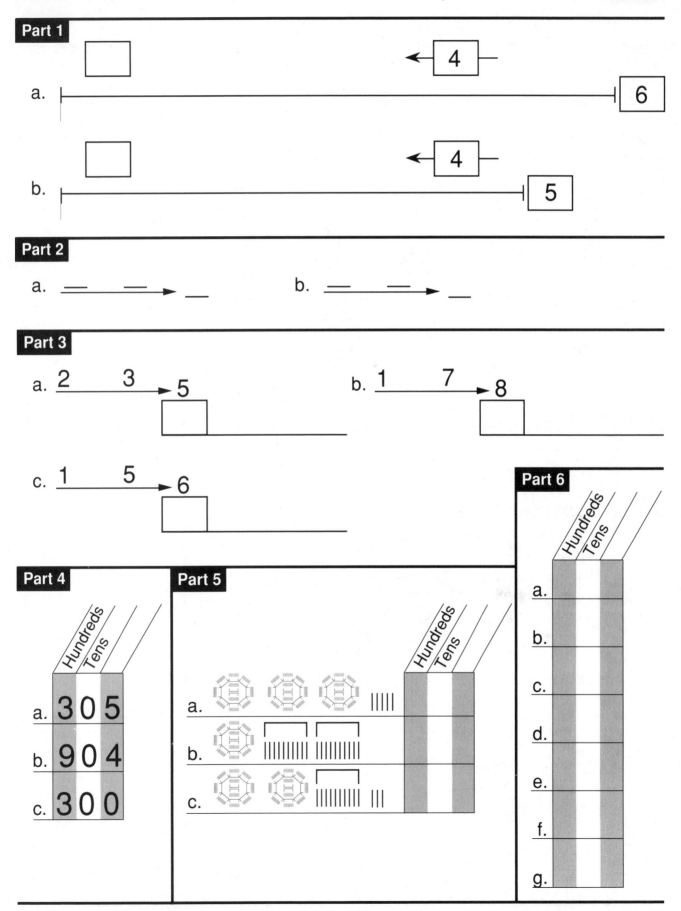

Part 1

a.

b.

Part 2

a.

b.

Part 3

a. 2 → 3 → 5

b. 1 → 7 → 8

c. 1 → 5 → 6

Part 4

Hundreds	Tens	
a. 3	0	5
b. 9	0	4
c. 3	0	0

Part 5

a.

b.

c.

Part 6

a.

b.

c.

d.

e.

f.

g.

71

Part 7

a. $\underset{}{2} \xrightarrow{8} \underline{}$

b. $\underset{}{2} \xrightarrow{6} \underline{}$

c. $\underset{}{2} \xrightarrow{10} \underline{}$

d. $\underset{}{2} \xrightarrow{4} \underline{}$

e. $\underset{}{2} \xrightarrow{2} \underline{}$

Part 8

a.
```
  7        7        7
+ 1      + 2      + 3
___      ___      ___
```

b.
```
  9        9        9
+ 1      + 2      + 3
___      ___      ___
```

Part 9

Tens

a. **1 2** How many groups of ten? ☐ How many leftovers? ☐

b. **8 3** How many groups of ten? ☐ How many leftovers? ☐

c. **5 1** How many groups of ten? ☐ How many leftovers? ☐

d. **1 1** How many groups of ten? ☐ How many leftovers? ☐

e. **7 6** How many groups of ten? ☐ How many leftovers? ☐

f. **2 1** How many groups of ten? ☐ How many leftovers? ☐

Part 10

a. $1 + 5 = \boxed{}$

b. $0 + 9 = \boxed{}$

c. $7 + 1 = \boxed{}$

d. $5 + 1 = \boxed{}$

e. $1 + 10 = \boxed{}$

f. $8 + 1 = \boxed{}$

g. $8 + 0 = \boxed{}$

h. $9 + 1 = \boxed{}$

Part 11

a. $1 \xrightarrow{\underline{}} 3$

b. $1 \xrightarrow{6} \underline{}$

c. $1 \xrightarrow{\underline{}} 9$

d. $1 \xrightarrow{\underline{}} 5$

e. $1 \xrightarrow{3} \underline{}$

f. $1 \xrightarrow{10} \underline{}$

g. $1 \xrightarrow{\underline{}} 4$

Lesson 34

Part 1

a. $=\!=\!\longrightarrow 6$ c. $=\!=\!\longrightarrow 4$

b. $=\!=\!\longrightarrow 9$ d. $=\!=\!\longrightarrow 8$

Part 2

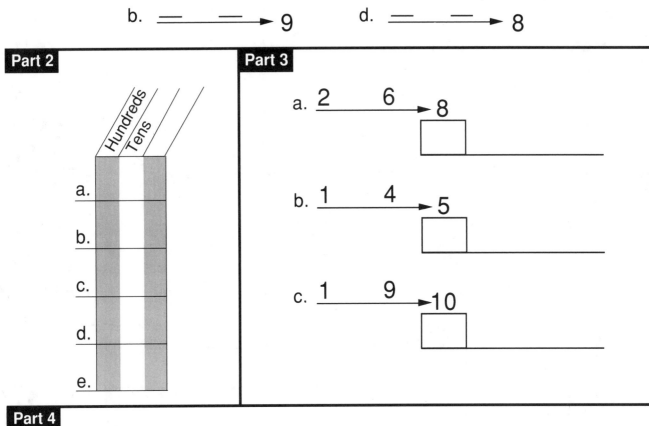

Part 3

a. $2 \quad 6 \longrightarrow 8$ ☐

b. $1 \quad 4 \longrightarrow 5$ ☐

c. $1 \quad 9 \longrightarrow 10$ ☐

Part 4

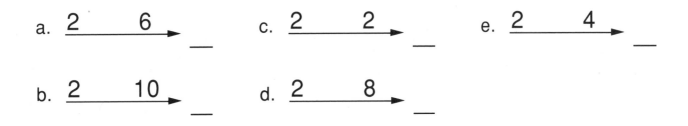

a. $2 \quad 6 \longrightarrow$ ___

b. $2 \quad 10 \longrightarrow$ ___

c. $2 \quad 2 \longrightarrow$ ___

d. $2 \quad 8 \longrightarrow$ ___

e. $2 \quad 4 \longrightarrow$ ___

Part 5

a. 6 leftovers

b. 1 group of ten + 6 leftovers

c. 6 groups of ten + 8 leftovers

d. 1 group of ten + 4 leftovers

e. 9 leftovers

Part 6

a. 3 7
  + 1 0

b. 5 1
  + 1 6

c. 5 0
  + 1 6

Part 7

a. 6 + 1 = ☐

6 + 2 = ☐

6 + __ = ☐

b. 5 + 1 = ☐

5 + 2 = ☐

5 + __ = ☐

Part 8

a. 10 + 1 = ☐

b. 8 + 1 = ☐

c. 0 + 9 = ☐

d. 9 + 1 = ☐

e. 6 + 1 = ☐

f. 4 + 1 = ☐

g. 4 + 0 = ☐

h. 1 + 5 = ☐

i. 1 + 10 = ☐

Part 9 Write the numbers for counting by 2.

Part 10 Write 2 addition facts for each number family.

a. 1 ──7──▶ 8

_____

_____

b. 1 ──10──▶ 11

_____

_____

Lesson 35

Part 1

a. $==$ $==$ → 5

b. $==$ $==$ → 11

c. $==$ $==$ → 3

d. $==$ $==$ → 7

Part 2

a. 3 groups of 100
+
7 groups of 10
+
4 leftovers

b. 8 groups of 100
+
No groups of 10
+
4 leftovers

c. 5 groups of 100
+
2 groups of 10
+
3 leftovers

d. 2 groups of 100
+
No groups of 10
+
2 leftovers

e. 6 groups of 100
+
3 groups of 10
+
No leftovers

Part 3

a. 1   6 → 7

b. 2   5 → 7

c. 1   3 → 4

Part 4

a. 3 6
  + 1 0

b. 1 8
  + 4 1

c. 7 0
  + 1 6

d. 5 1
  + 1 7

Part 5

a. 2   6 → __

b. 2   10 → __

c. 2   4 → __

d. 2   8 → __

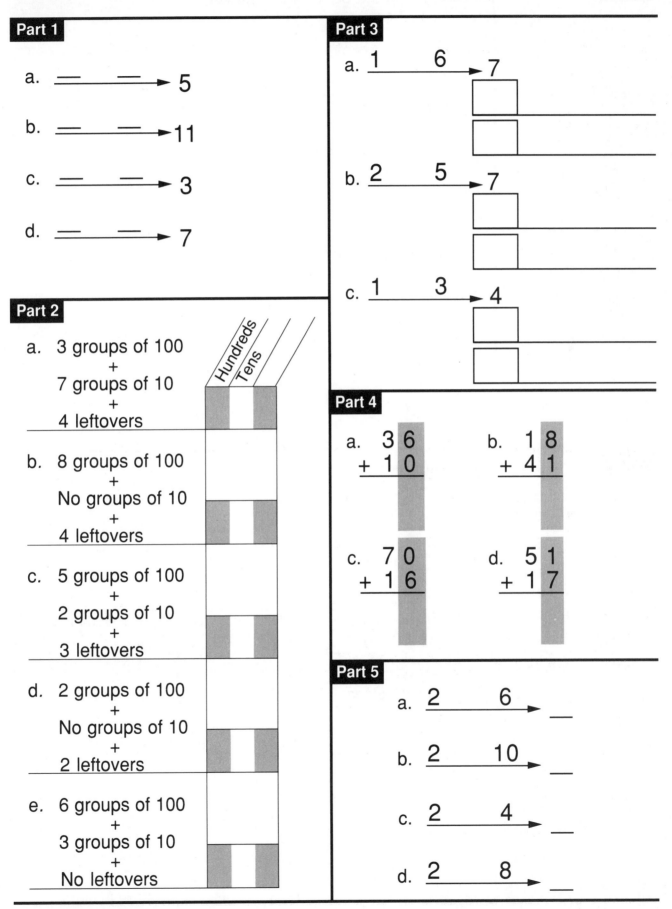

Hundreds	Tens	
a.		
b.		
c.		
d.		
e.		

Part 7

Complete each sign:

≥ = ≤

a. 25 — 24

b. 27 — 26

c. 27 — 28

d. 28 — 28

a. 5 + 1 = ☐

b. 1 + 6 = ☐

c. 2 + 0 = ☐

d. 7 + 1 = ☐

e. 0 + 10 = ☐

f. 1 + 8 = ☐

Part 8 Write the number problems.

a. You have 8 coins. Then you lose 6 coins. How many coins do you end up with?

___ ___ ___

b. You have 6 dolls. Then you buy 4 more dolls. How many dolls do you end up with?

___ ___ ___

c. You have 9 pens. Then you sell 8 pens. How many pens do you end up with?

___ ___ ___

Lesson 36

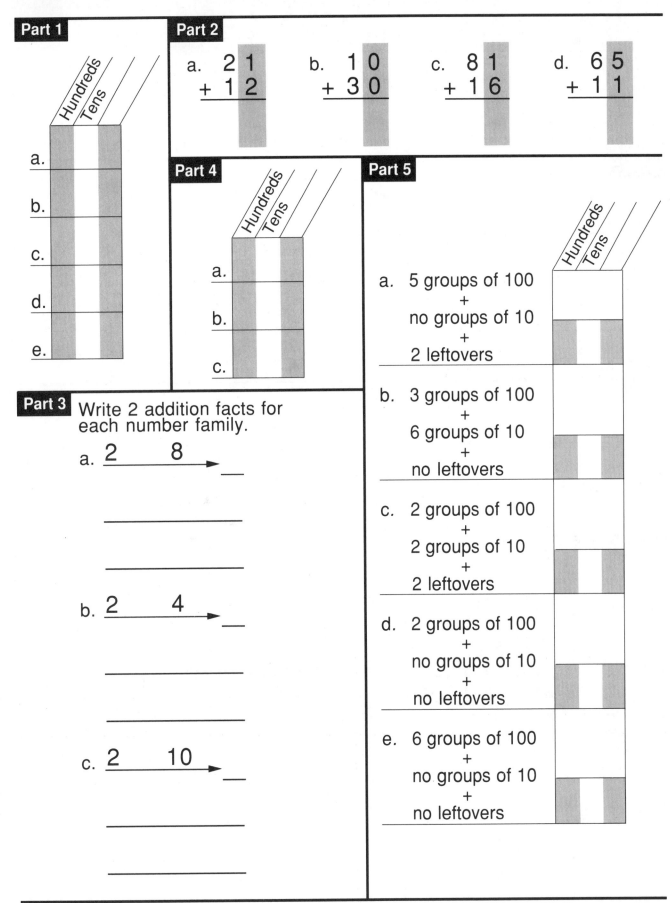

Part 1

Hundreds / Tens

a.

b.

c.

d.

e.

Part 2

a. 2 1
   + 1 2

b. 1 0
   + 3 0

c. 8 1
   + 1 6

d. 6 5
   + 1 1

Part 4

Hundreds / Tens

a.

b.

c.

Part 3 Write 2 addition facts for each number family.

a. 2 _____ 8 → ___

_____

_____

b. 2 _____ 4 → ___

_____

_____

c. 2 _____ 10 → ___

_____

_____

Part 5

Hundreds / Tens

a. 5 groups of 100
    +
    no groups of 10
    +
    2 leftovers

b. 3 groups of 100
    +
    6 groups of 10
    +
    no leftovers

c. 2 groups of 100
    +
    2 groups of 10
    +
    2 leftovers

d. 2 groups of 100
    +
    no groups of 10
    +
    no leftovers

e. 6 groups of 100
    +
    no groups of 10
    +
    no leftovers

Part 6 Write 2 subtraction facts for each number family.

a. $\xrightarrow[\quad\quad]{2\qquad 8} 10$ b. $\xrightarrow[\quad\quad]{1\qquad 5} 6$

_____   _____

_____   _____

Part 7

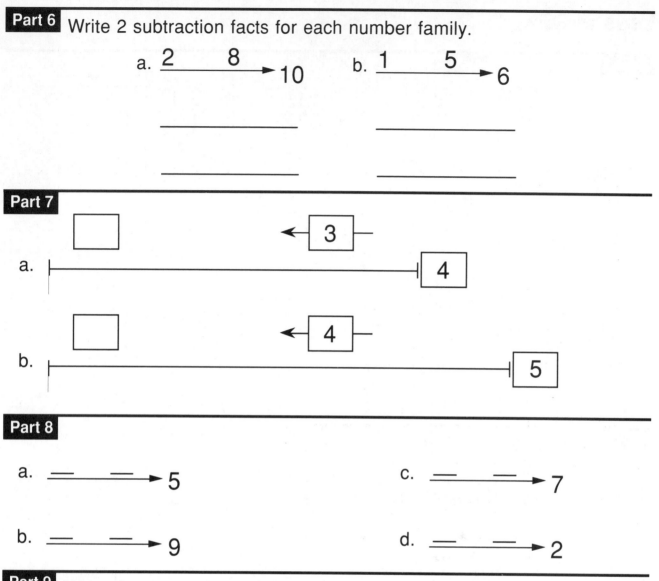

a. [ ] $\leftarrow$ [3]   [4]

b. [ ] $\leftarrow$ [4]   [5]

Part 8

a. $\overset{=\ \ =}{\xrightarrow{\quad\quad}} 5$ c. $\overset{=\ \ =}{\xrightarrow{\quad\quad}} 7$

b. $\overset{=\ \ =}{\xrightarrow{\quad\quad}} 9$ d. $\overset{=\ \ =}{\xrightarrow{\quad\quad}} 2$

Part 9 Write the number problems.

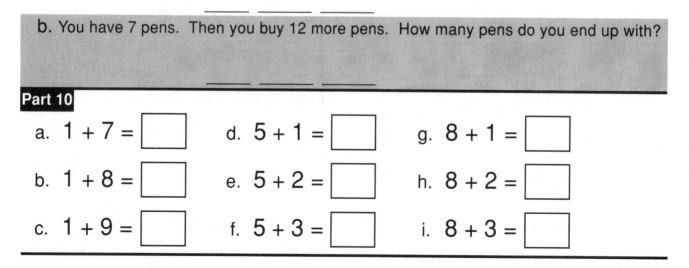

a. You have 13 pets. Then you sell 6 pets. How many pets do you end up with?

_____ _____ _____

b. You have 7 pens. Then you buy 12 more pens. How many pens do you end up with?

_____ _____ _____

Part 10

a. $1 + 7 =$ [ ]   d. $5 + 1 =$ [ ]   g. $8 + 1 =$ [ ]

b. $1 + 8 =$ [ ]   e. $5 + 2 =$ [ ]   h. $8 + 2 =$ [ ]

c. $1 + 9 =$ [ ]   f. $5 + 3 =$ [ ]   i. $8 + 3 =$ [ ]

Lesson 37

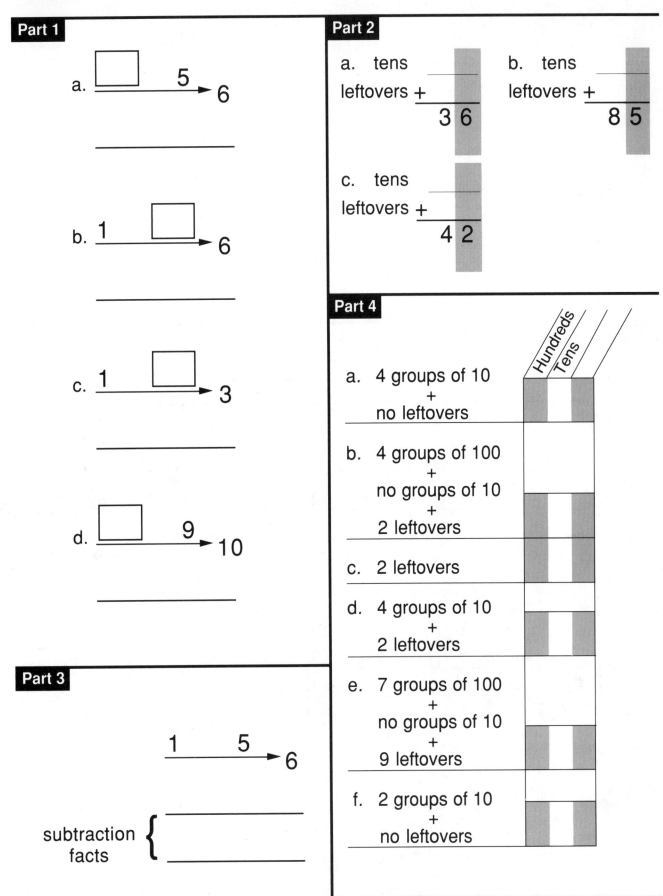

Part 1

a. [ ] →5→ 6

_____

b. 1 [ ] →6

_____

c. 1 [ ] →3

_____

d. [ ] →9→ 10

_____

Part 2

a. tens
   leftovers + ____
   _____
        3 | 6

b. tens
   leftovers + ____
   _____
        8 | 5

c. tens
   leftovers + ____
   _____
        4 | 2

Part 3

1 →5→ 6

subtraction { _____
facts   _____

Part 4

		Hundreds	Tens	
a. 4 groups of 10 + no leftovers				
b. 4 groups of 100 + no groups of 10 + 2 leftovers				
c. 2 leftovers				
d. 4 groups of 10 + 2 leftovers				
e. 7 groups of 100 + no groups of 10 + 9 leftovers				
f. 2 groups of 10 + no leftovers				

Part 5 Write 2 addition facts for each number family.

a. 2 ———→ 6 ———
_____

_____

b. 2 ———→ 4 ———
_____

_____

c. 2 ———→ 10 ———
_____

_____

d. 2 ———→ 8 ———
_____

_____

Part 6

a. — ———→ 6   b. — ———→ 10   c. — ———→ 4

Part 7

a.
```
  3 6
+ 1 0
─────
```

b.
```
  5 8
+ 1 0
─────
```

c.
```
  3 1
+ 1 0
─────
```

d.
```
  1 0
+ 5 2
─────
```

e.
```
  1 0
+ 1 3
─────
```

Lesson 38

Part 1

a. ☐ —6→ 7

_____

c. 1 ☐ —→ 5

_____

b. 1 ☐ —→ 4

_____

d. ☐ —10→ 11

_____

Part 2

a.
```
  +
5 8
```

b.
```
  +
9 2
```

c.
```
  +
6 7
```

d.
```
  +
1 7
```

Part 3

1 —5→ 6

addition facts { _____ _____

subtraction facts { _____ _____

Part 4

		Hundreds	Tens	
a.	5 groups of 10 + no leftovers			
b.	3 groups of 100 + no groups of 10 + no leftovers			
c.	5 leftovers			
d.	6 groups of 100 + no groups of 10 + 4 leftovers			
e.	7 groups of 100 + 5 groups of 10 + no leftovers			
f.	1 group of 10 + 2 leftovers			

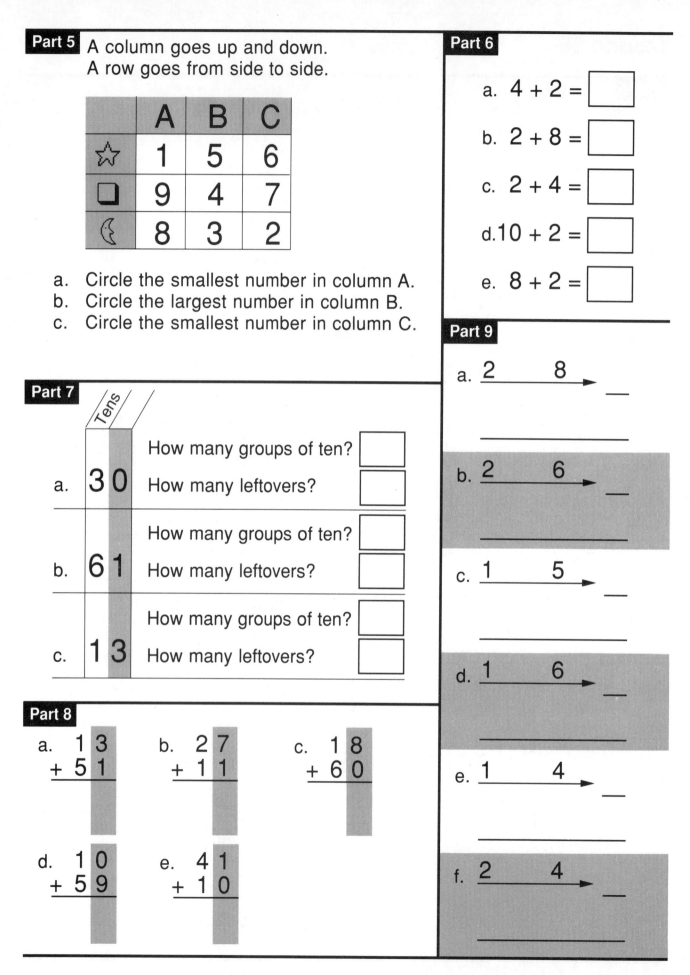

Part 5 A column goes up and down.
A row goes from side to side.

	A	B	C
☆	1	5	6
▢	9	4	7
☾	8	3	2

a. Circle the smallest number in column A.
b. Circle the largest number in column B.
c. Circle the smallest number in column C.

Part 6

a. 4 + 2 = ☐

b. 2 + 8 = ☐

c. 2 + 4 = ☐

d. 10 + 2 = ☐

e. 8 + 2 = ☐

Part 7

Tens

a. **3 0** How many groups of ten? ☐
How many leftovers? ☐

b. **6 1** How many groups of ten? ☐
How many leftovers? ☐

c. **1 3** How many groups of ten? ☐
How many leftovers? ☐

Part 9

a. 2   8
___

b. 2   6
___

c. 1   5
___

d. 1   6
___

e. 1   4
___

f. 2   4
___

Part 8

a. 1 **3**
  + 5 **1**
  _____

b. 2 **7**
  + 1 **1**
  _____

c. 1 **8**
  + 6 **0**
  _____

d. 1 **0**
  + 5 **9**
  _____

e. 4 **1**
  + 1 **0**
  _____

82

Lesson 39

Part 1

a. 2 + 10 = ⬜ _

b. 6 + 2 = ⬜ _

c. 8 + 2 = ⬜ _

d. 2 + 6 = ⬜ _

e. 10 + 2 = ⬜ _

Part 2

a. 1 ⬜ → 8

b. 1 ⬜ → 9

c. ⬜ 4 → 5

d. ⬜ 9 → 10

Part 3

A column goes up and down.
A row goes from side to side.

	☕	🌙	☆
A	12	11	10
B	5	6	7
C	2	10	9

a. Circle the smallest number in row A.

b. Circle the smallest number in row C.

c. Circle the largest number in row B.

Part 4

1 9 → 10

addition facts { _____ _____

subtraction facts { _____ _____

Part 5

a. +
____
    1 9

b. +
____
    1 3

c. +
____
    2 6

83

Part 6

a. $\underrightarrow{1 \quad -} 10$

c. $\underrightarrow{1 \quad -} 4$

b. $\underrightarrow{1 \quad -} 6$

d. $\underrightarrow{1 \quad -} 9$

Part 7 Write the number problems.

a. You have 13 cups. Then you find 12 more cups. How many cups do you end up with?

_____

b. You run 3 miles. Then you run 6 more miles. How many miles do you end up running?

_____

c. You have 14 pets. Then you sell 6 pets. How many pets do you end up with?

_____

Part 8

a.
```
  1 5
+ 3 1
```

b.
```
  1 9
+ 4 0
```

c.
```
  5 0
+ 1 7
```

d.
```
  8 0
+ 1 0
```

e.
```
  3 0
+ 1 0
```

f.
```
  1 0
+ 5 6
```

Part 9 Complete each sign:

$\geqslant = \leqslant$

a. 41 — 40

b. 36 — 40

c. 39 — 40

Part 10

a.
```
  7
+ 1
```
```
  7
+ 2
```
```
  7
+ 3
```

b.
```
  4
+ 1
```
```
  4
+ 2
```
```
  4
+ 3
```

c.
```
  8
+ 1
```
```
  8
+ 2
```
```
  8
+ 3
```

Lesson 40

Part 1

a. 1 [ ] → 6

b. [ ] 3 → 4

c. 1 [ ] → 9

d. 1 [ ] → 7

e. [ ] 9 → 10

Part 2

5	10
15	20
25	30

Part 3

	Hundreds	Tens		
a.	6	4	1	How many groups of 100? [ ] How many groups of 10? [ ] How many leftovers? [ ]
b.		5	0	How many groups of 10? [ ] How many leftovers? [ ]
c.	5	7	0	How many groups of 100? [ ] How many groups of 10? [ ] How many leftovers? [ ]
d.	3	0	2	How many groups of 100? [ ] How many groups of 10? [ ] How many leftovers? [ ]
e.	1	0	0	How many groups of 100? [ ] How many groups of 10? [ ] How many leftovers? [ ]

Part 4

a. $10 + 2 =$ [ ] __

b. $2 + 2 =$ [ ] __

c. $4 + 2 =$ [ ] __

d. $2 + 6 =$ [ ] __

e. $8 + 2 =$ [ ] __

f. $2 + 4 =$ [ ] __

g. $2 + 10 =$ [ ] __

h. $6 + 2 =$ [ ] __

i. $2 + 8 =$ [ ] __

Part 5 A column goes up and down.
A row goes from side to side.

	A	B	C	D
🌹	4	6	8	10
☕	2	10	3	1
☆	9	7	6	8

a. Circle the smallest number in column A.
b. Circle the smallest number in column D.
c. Circle the smallest number in the star row.
d. Circle the largest number in the flower row.

Part 6

$$1 \qquad 6 \rightarrow 7$$

addition facts { _____
                  _____

subtraction facts { _____
                     _____

Part 7

a. 3 0
  +   8

b. 7 0
  +   4

c. 5 0
  +   9

d. 2 0
  +   3

Part 8

a. +
     5 6

b. +
     3 9

c. +
     2 6

d. +
     1 3

Part 9

a. 4 6
  + 1 2

b. 1 7
  + 2 1

c. 2 0
  + 6 0

d. 8 2
  + 1 6

e. 1 4
  + 1 2

f. 1 1
  + 8 2

Part 10 Write all the numbers for counting by 2.

___ ___ ___ ___ ___ ___ ___ ___ ___ ___

Test Lesson 4   Test 4

Part 1

a. $7 - 6 = \boxed{}$

b. $9 - 8 = \boxed{}$

c. $7 - 1 = \boxed{}$

d. $4 - 1 = \boxed{}$

e. $10 - 9 = \boxed{}$

f. $10 - 1 = \boxed{}$

Part 1

a. $8 + 2 = \boxed{}$

b. $2 + 4 = \boxed{}$

c. $10 + 2 = \boxed{}$

d. $2 + 8 = \boxed{}$

e. $6 + 2 = \boxed{}$

f. $4 + 2 = \boxed{}$

Part 2

Hundreds / Tens

a.

b.

c.

Part 4 Write each numeral.

Hundreds / Tens

a. 6 groups of 100
    +
    no groups of 10
    +
    no leftovers

b. 3 groups of 10
    +
    no leftovers

c. 1 group of 10
    +
    2 leftovers

d. 4 groups of 100
    +
    no groups of 10
    +
    no leftovers

Part 3 Write the place-value addition for each number.

a.
$$+ $$
$$1\ 6$$

b.
$$+ $$
$$9\ 4$$

Part 5 Write the facts.

$$1 \quad\xrightarrow{}\quad 9 \longrightarrow 10$$

addition
facts $\Big\{$ _____
_____

subtraction
facts $\Big\{$ _____
_____

87

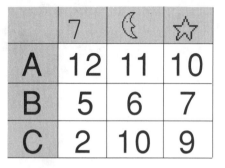

	7	☾	☆
A	12	11	10
B	5	6	7
C	2	10	9

a. Circle the smallest number in row C.

b. Circle the smallest number in row A.

c. Circle the largest number in row B.

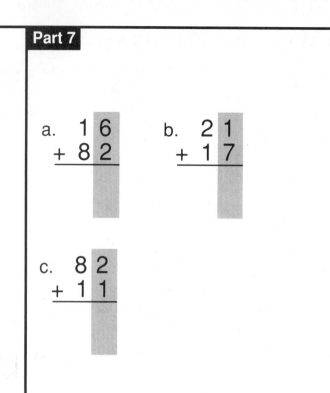

a.
```
  1 6
+ 8 2
```

b.
```
  2 1
+ 1 7
```

c.
```
  8 2
+ 1 1
```

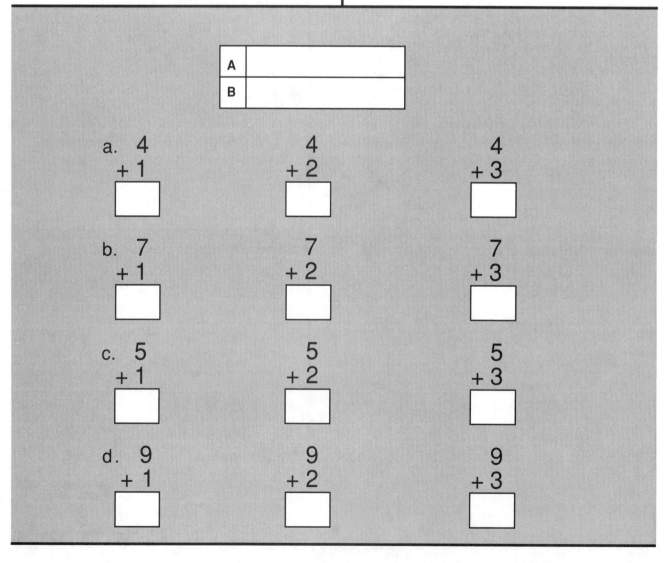

A	
B	

a.
```
  4
+ 1
```
```
  4
+ 2
```
```
  4
+ 3
```

b.
```
  7
+ 1
```
```
  7
+ 2
```
```
  7
+ 3
```

c.
```
  5
+ 1
```
```
  5
+ 2
```
```
  5
+ 3
```

d.
```
  9
+ 1
```
```
  9
+ 2
```
```
  9
+ 3
```

Test 4/Extra Practice

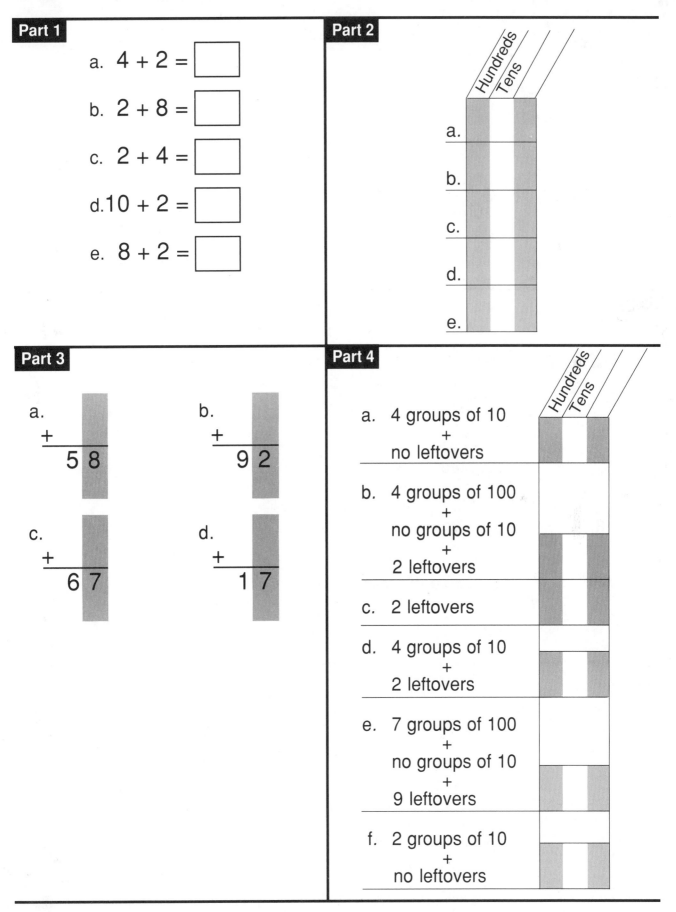

Part 1

a. $4 + 2 =$ ☐

b. $2 + 8 =$ ☐

c. $2 + 4 =$ ☐

d. $10 + 2 =$ ☐

e. $8 + 2 =$ ☐

Part 2

Hundreds Tens

a.

b.

c.

d.

e.

Part 3

a.
```
+
  5 8
```

b.
```
+
  9 2
```

c.
```
+
  6 7
```

d.
```
+
  1 7
```

Part 4

Hundreds Tens

a. 4 groups of 10
   +
   no leftovers

b. 4 groups of 100
   +
   no groups of 10
   +
   2 leftovers

c. 2 leftovers

d. 4 groups of 10
   +
   2 leftovers

e. 7 groups of 100
   +
   no groups of 10
   +
   9 leftovers

f. 2 groups of 10
   +
   no leftovers

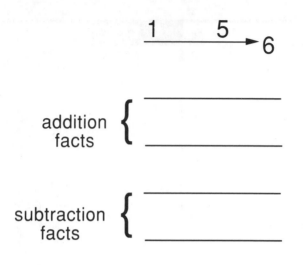

$$\underrightarrow{1 \qquad 5} 6$$

addition
facts
{ _____

_____

subtraction
facts
{ _____

_____

Part 6

A column goes up and down.
A row goes from side to side.

	A	B	C
☆	1	5	6
❑	9	4	7
☾	8	3	2

a. Circle the smallest number in column A.
b. Circle the largest number in column B.
c. Circle the smallest number in column C.

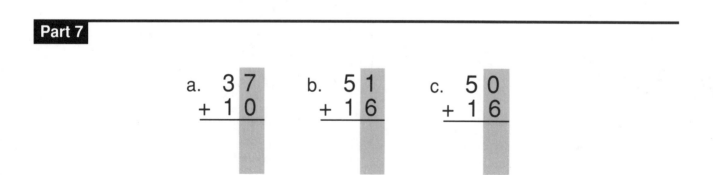

a. 3 7
  + 1 0
  ‾‾‾‾‾

b. 5 1
  + 1 6
  ‾‾‾‾‾

c. 5 0
  + 1 6
  ‾‾‾‾‾

Lesson 41

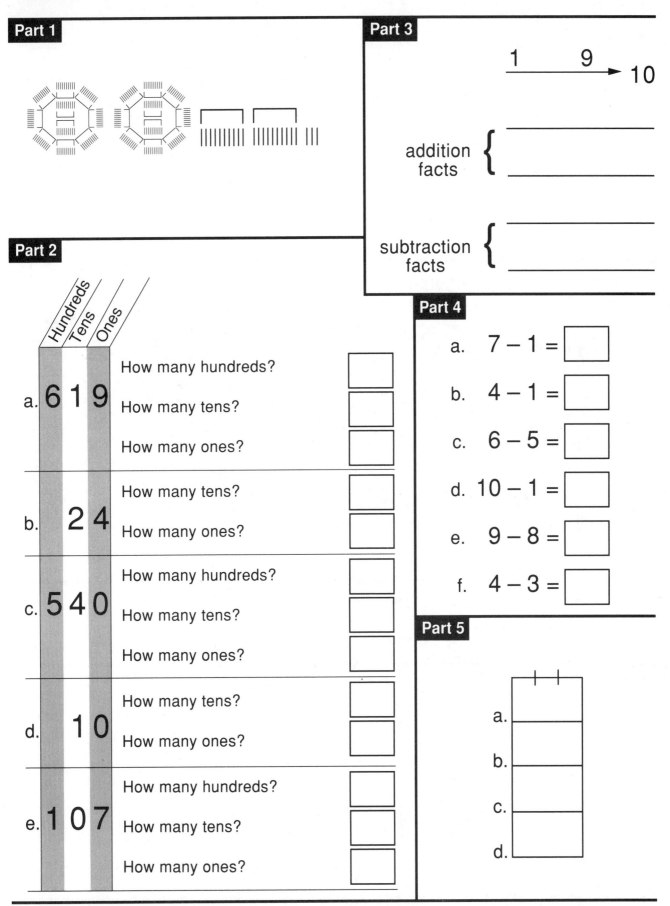

Part 1

Part 2

	Hundreds	Tens	Ones		
a.	6	1	9	How many hundreds?	
				How many tens?	
				How many ones?	
b.		2	4	How many tens?	
				How many ones?	
c.	5	4	0	How many hundreds?	
				How many tens?	
				How many ones?	
d.		1	0	How many tens?	
				How many ones?	
e.	1	0	7	How many hundreds?	
				How many tens?	
				How many ones?	

Part 3

$$1 \quad\quad 9 \longrightarrow 10$$

addition facts {

_____

_____

subtraction facts {

_____

_____

Part 4

a. $7 - 1 = \boxed{}$

b. $4 - 1 = \boxed{}$

c. $6 - 5 = \boxed{}$

d. $10 - 1 = \boxed{}$

e. $9 - 8 = \boxed{}$

f. $4 - 3 = \boxed{}$

Part 5

a.

b.

c.

d.

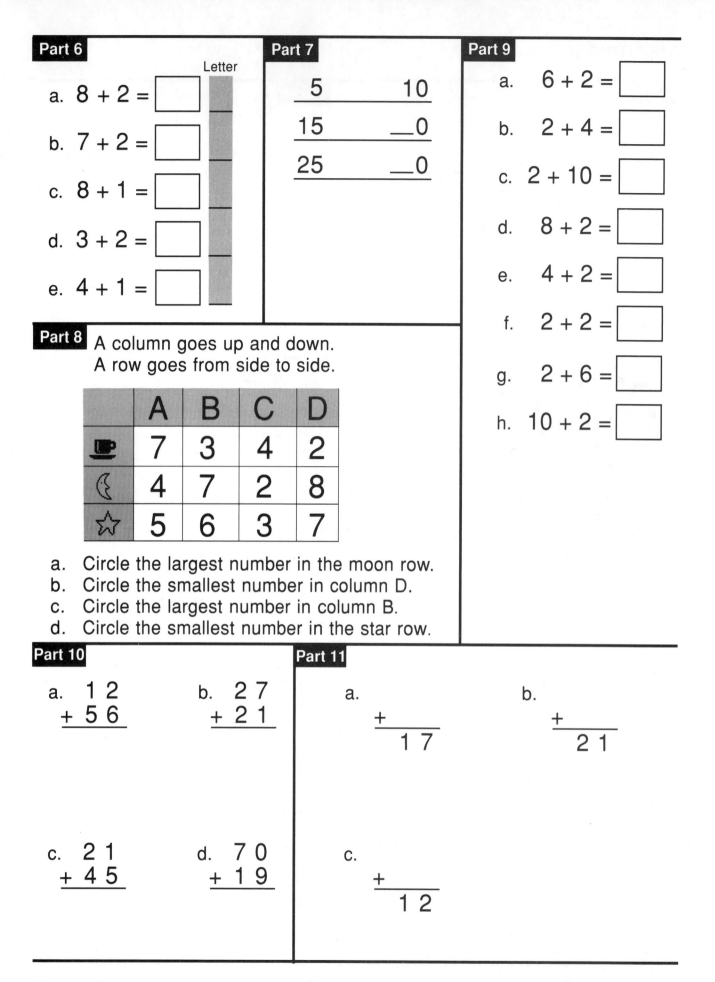

Part 6

Letter

a. 8 + 2 = ☐

b. 7 + 2 = ☐

c. 8 + 1 = ☐

d. 3 + 2 = ☐

e. 4 + 1 = ☐

Part 7

5   10

15   _0

25   _0

Part 9

a. 6 + 2 = ☐

b. 2 + 4 = ☐

c. 2 + 10 = ☐

d. 8 + 2 = ☐

e. 4 + 2 = ☐

f. 2 + 2 = ☐

g. 2 + 6 = ☐

h. 10 + 2 = ☐

Part 8 A column goes up and down.
A row goes from side to side.

	A	B	C	D
☕	7	3	4	2
☾	4	7	2	8
☆	5	6	3	7

a. Circle the largest number in the moon row.
b. Circle the smallest number in column D.
c. Circle the largest number in column B.
d. Circle the smallest number in the star row.

Part 10

a.   1 2
  + 5 6

b.   2 7
  + 2 1

c.   2 1
  + 4 5

d.   7 0
  + 1 9

Part 11

a.
  +
    1 7

b.
  +
    2 1

c.
  +
    1 2

Lesson 42

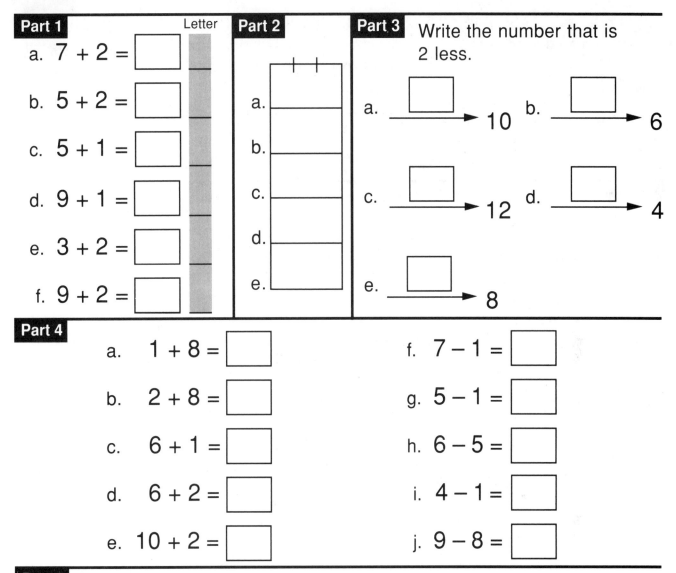

Part 1   Letter

a. $7 + 2 =$ ☐

b. $5 + 2 =$ ☐

c. $5 + 1 =$ ☐

d. $9 + 1 =$ ☐

e. $3 + 2 =$ ☐

f. $9 + 2 =$ ☐

Part 2

a.

b.

c.

d.

e.

Part 3 Write the number that is 2 less.

a. ☐ ⟶ 10

b. ☐ ⟶ 6

c. ☐ ⟶ 12

d. ☐ ⟶ 4

e. ☐ ⟶ 8

Part 4

a. $1 + 8 =$ ☐

b. $2 + 8 =$ ☐

c. $6 + 1 =$ ☐

d. $6 + 2 =$ ☐

e. $10 + 2 =$ ☐

f. $7 - 1 =$ ☐

g. $5 - 1 =$ ☐

h. $6 - 5 =$ ☐

i. $4 - 1 =$ ☐

j. $9 - 8 =$ ☐

Part 5

a. You have 6 dogs. You find 2 more dogs. How many dogs do you end up with?

_____

b. You have 6 rings. You lose 1 ring. How many rings do you end up with?

_____

c. You have 10 pens. You sell 1 pen. How many pens do you end up with?

_____

d. You have 4 cups. You make 2 more cups. How many cups do you end up with?

_____

	5 years	10 years	15 years
Oak tree			
Elm tree	Y		
Pine tree			X

a. **Which tree** does **X** tell about? _____

b. **How many years** does **X** tell about? _____

c. **Which tree** does **Y** tell about? _____

d. **How many years** does **Y** tell about? _____

Part 7

a. 1 6
  + 6 2

b. 2 8
  + 4 1

c. 1 0
  + 7 9

d. 1 2
  + 5 2

e. 2 4
  + 4 2

Part 8

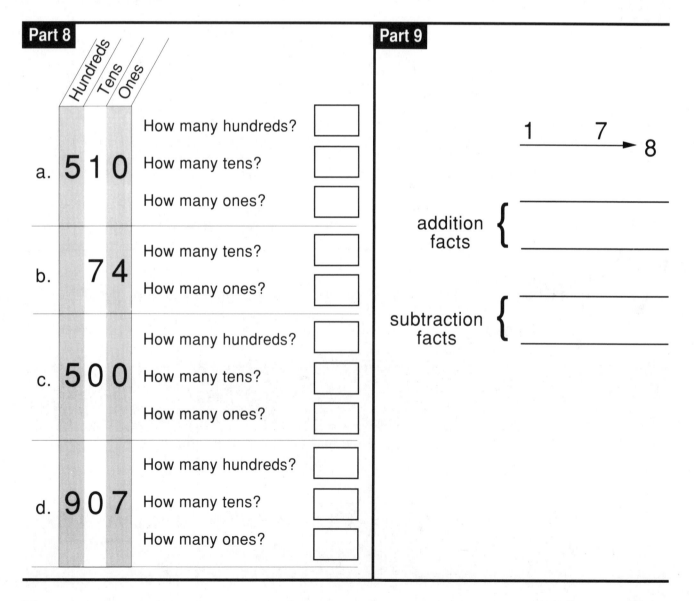

Hundreds Tens Ones

a. **5 1 0**

How many hundreds? ☐

How many tens? ☐

How many ones? ☐

b. **7 4**

How many tens? ☐

How many ones? ☐

c. **5 0 0**

How many hundreds? ☐

How many tens? ☐

How many ones? ☐

d. **9 0 7**

How many hundreds? ☐

How many tens? ☐

How many ones? ☐

Part 9

1   7 ⟶ 8

addition facts { _____
          _____

subtraction facts { _____
          _____

Lesson 43

Part 1

a. $5 - 2 =$ ▢

b. $8 - 1 =$ ▢

c. $6 - 2 =$ ▢

d. $12 - 2 =$ ▢

e. $10 - 1 =$ ▢

f. $6 - 1 =$ ▢

Part 2

a. 5 hundreds + no tens + no ones

b. 4 tens + 6 ones

c. 9 hundreds + no tens + 3 ones

d. 7 ones

e. 1 ten + 2 ones

Part 3

```
    5      _0
   _5      _0
   _5      _0
   _5      _0
   45      50
```

Part 4

a. You have 4 pens. You buy 2 more pens. How many pens do you end up with?

_____

b. You have 7 cars. You sell 1 car. How many cars do you end up with?

_____

c. You have 9 books. You lose 1 book. How many books do you end up with?

_____

d. You have 8 cats. You find 1 more cat. How many cats do you end up with?

_____

	5 years	10 years	15 years
Elm tree	Z	Y	
Pine tree			X
Oak tree			

a. **Which tree** does **Y** tell about? _____

b. **How many years** does **Y** tell about? _____

c. **Which tree** does **X** tell about? _____

d. **How many years** does **X** tell about? _____

e. **Which tree** does **Z** tell about? _____

f. **How many years** does **Z** tell about? _____

Part 6

a. $10 - 1 = \boxed{}$

b. $6 - 5 = \boxed{}$

c. $4 - 1 = \boxed{}$

d. $9 - 8 = \boxed{}$

e. $5 - 1 = \boxed{}$

f. $2 + 8 = \boxed{}$

g. $1 + 7 = \boxed{}$

h. $6 + 2 = \boxed{}$

i. $8 + 1 = \boxed{}$

j. $2 + 4 = \boxed{}$

Part 7 Write the number that is 2 less.

a. $\boxed{} \longrightarrow 8$

b. $\boxed{} \longrightarrow 6$

c. $\boxed{} \longrightarrow 4$

d. $\boxed{} \longrightarrow 10$

e. $\boxed{} \longrightarrow 12$

Part 8

a. $\begin{array}{r} 28 \\ + 41 \\ \hline \end{array}$
b. $\begin{array}{r} 66 \\ + 10 \\ \hline \end{array}$
c. $\begin{array}{r} 28 \\ + 21 \\ \hline \end{array}$
d. $\begin{array}{r} 26 \\ + 41 \\ \hline \end{array}$
e. $\begin{array}{r} 17 \\ + 60 \\ \hline \end{array}$
f. $\begin{array}{r} 74 \\ + 12 \\ \hline \end{array}$

Lesson 44

Part 1
Write the number that is 2 less.

a. ☐ ⟶ 12

b. ☐ ⟶ 4

c. ☐ ⟶ 8

d. ☐ ⟶ 6

e. ☐ ⟶ 10

Part 2

a. 2 —— ⟶ 6

b. 2 —— ⟶ 12

c. 2 —— ⟶ 4

d. 2 —— ⟶ 10

e. 2 —— ⟶ 8

Part 3

a. $10 - 1 = $ ☐

b. $10 - 2 = $ ☐

c. $6 - 2 = $ ☐

d. $7 - 1 = $ ☐

e. $5 - 1 = $ ☐

f. $5 - 2 = $ ☐

Part 4

5 ——

—— ——

—— 30

—— 40

—— 50

Part 5

	5 years	10 years	15 years
Pine tree	8	12	19
Oak tree	6	11	16
Elm tree	7	14	18

a. Oak tree at 15 years? _____

b. Elm tree at 5 years? _____

c. Oak tree at 5 years? _____

d. Pine tree at 10 years? _____

Part 6

a. $2 + 8 =$ ☐

b. $5 + 1 =$ ☐

c. $2 + 10 =$ ☐

d. $6 + 2 =$ ☐

e. $1 + 8 =$ ☐

f. $4 - 1 =$ ☐

g. $9 - 8 =$ ☐

h. $5 - 1 =$ ☐

i. $6 - 5 =$ ☐

j. $10 - 1 =$ ☐

Part 7

a. 563
How many tens? ☐
How many hundreds? ☐

b. 390
How many hundreds? ☐
How many ones? ☐

c. 903
How many ones? ☐
How many tens? ☐

Part 8 Write the number problems and the answers.

a. You have 6 cups. You find 2 more cups. How many cups do you end up with?

_____

b. Tom has 4 dogs. He sells 1 dog. How many dogs does he end up with?

_____

Part 9

a.
```
  1 4
+ 3 2
```

b.
```
  2 0
+ 1 7
```

c.
```
  1 2
+ 8 4
```

Lesson 45

a. 7
   − 0

b. 6
   − 0

c. 2
   − 1

d. 4
   − 1

e. 4
   − 0

f. 9
   − 1

Part 2

5 _____

_____ _____

_____ 30

_____ _____

_____ 50

Part 3

a. 5 − 2 = ☐

b. 8 + 2 = ☐

c. 4 + 2 = ☐

d. 10 − 1 = ☐

e. 7 − 2 = ☐

f. 4 + 1 = ☐

Part 4

a.
A boy had 6 shoes.
He lost 1 shoe.
How many shoes did
he end up with?

   6
 − 1
 ☐

c.
A boy has 9 goats.
He sells 1 goat.
How many goats does
he end up with?

b.
A boy had 4 cups.
He made 2 more cups.
How many cups did
he end up with?

d.
A boy has 8 coins.
He finds 2 more coins.
How many coins does
he end up with?

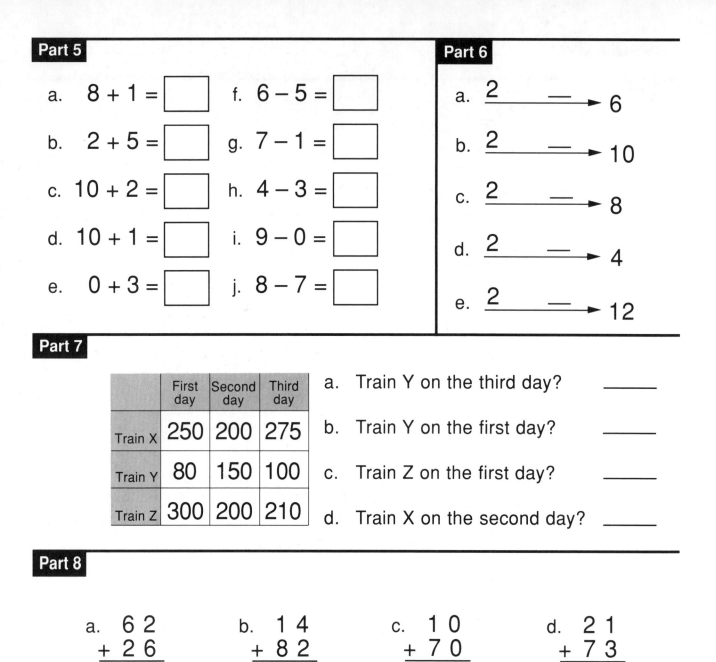

Part 5

a. 8 + 1 = ☐　　f. 6 − 5 = ☐

b. 2 + 5 = ☐　　g. 7 − 1 = ☐

c. 10 + 2 = ☐　　h. 4 − 3 = ☐

d. 10 + 1 = ☐　　i. 9 − 0 = ☐

e. 0 + 3 = ☐　　j. 8 − 7 = ☐

Part 6

a. 2 ———→ 6

b. 2 ———→ 10

c. 2 ———→ 8

d. 2 ———→ 4

e. 2 ———→ 12

Part 7

	First day	Second day	Third day
Train X	250	200	275
Train Y	80	150	100
Train Z	300	200	210

a. Train Y on the third day? _____

b. Train Y on the first day? _____

c. Train Z on the first day? _____

d. Train X on the second day? _____

Part 8

a. 　6 2
　+ 2 6

b. 　1 4
　+ 8 2

c. 　1 0
　+ 7 0

d. 　2 1
　+ 7 3

Lesson 46

Part 1

a. $6 + 1 = \boxed{}$

b. $6 - 1 = \boxed{}$

c. $8 - 2 = \boxed{}$

d. $4 + 1 = \boxed{}$

e. $4 + 2 = \boxed{}$

f. $6 - 2 = \boxed{}$

Part 2

$$2 \qquad 6 \longrightarrow 8$$

_____

_____

Part 3

a. $10 - 8 = \boxed{}$

b. $6 - 4 = \boxed{}$

c. $12 - 10 = \boxed{}$

d. $8 - 6 = \boxed{}$

e. $10 - 2 = \boxed{}$

f. $6 - 2 = \boxed{}$

g. $12 - 2 = \boxed{}$

h. $8 - 2 = \boxed{}$

Part 4

Part 5

a.
A girl makes 8 cups.
Then she makes 2 more cups.
How many cups does she end up with?

b.
A girl has 6 coins.
She loses 1 coin.
How many coins does she end up with?

c.
A girl has 10 shoes.
She gets rid of 1 shoe.
How many shoes does she end up with?

d.
A girl has 2 bikes.
She buys 2 more bikes.
How many bikes does she end up with?

Part 6

a. $10 - 8 =$ ☐

b. $6 - 2 =$ ☐

c. $10 - 2 =$ ☐

d. $12 - 2 =$ ☐

e. $6 - 4 =$ ☐

f. $8 - 6 =$ ☐

g. $8 - 2 =$ ☐

h. $4 - 2 =$ ☐

Part 7

	First day	Second day	Third day
Car A	150	400	275
Car B	400	401	399
Car C	275	310	305

a. Car A on the second day? _____

b. Car A on the third day? _____

c. Car C on the first day? _____

d. Car B on the second day? _____

Part 8

a. $10 + 2 =$ ☐   e. $9 - 1 =$ ☐

b. $2 + 6 =$ ☐   f. $4 - 3 =$ ☐

c. $1 + 4 =$ ☐   g. $8 - 7 =$ ☐

d. $2 + 8 =$ ☐   h. $10 - 1 =$ ☐

Part 9

a. 3 6 1   How many tens? ☐   How many ones? ☐

b. 4 0 3   How many hundreds? ☐   How many tens? ☐

c. 9 2 8   How many hundreds? ☐   How many tens? ☐

Part 10 Write all the numbers for counting by 2.

— — — — — — — — — — — —

Write the place-value addition.

a.
```
  +
 3 6
```

b.
```
  +
 1 9
```

Part 12

a. 2 ——→ 8   d. 1 ——→ 3

b. 2 ——→ 12   e. 2 ——→ 4

c. 1 ——→ 9   f. 1 ——→ 6

Part 13

a.
```
   9     9     9
 + 1   + 2   + 3
```

b.
```
   8     8     8
 + 1   + 2   + 3
```

c.
```
   7     7     7
 + 1   + 2   + 3
```

Part 14

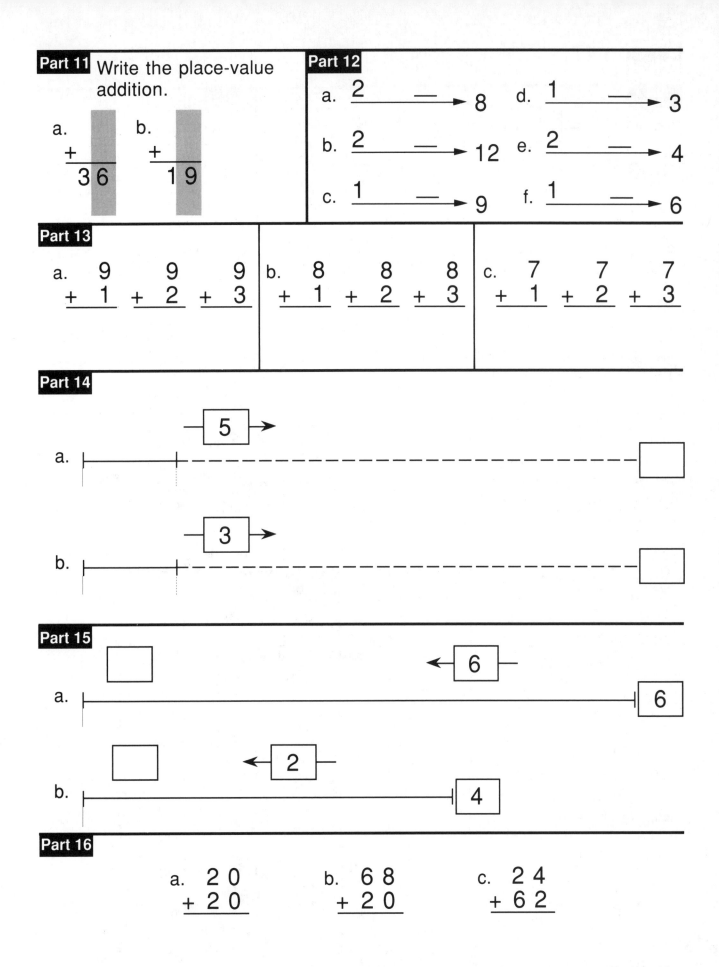

a. ⊢————┼— 5 →— - - - - - - - - - - - - - - - □

b. ⊢————┼— 3 →— - - - - - - - - - - - - - - - □

Part 15

a. □   ←[6]⊣   ⊢————————————————⊣ [6]

b. □   ←[2]⊣   ⊢——————————⊣ [4]

Part 16

a.
```
  2 0
+ 2 0
```

b.
```
  6 8
+ 2 0
```

c.
```
  2 4
+ 6 2
```

Lesson 47

Part 1

a. $6 - 1 = \boxed{}$

b. $3 - 1 = \boxed{}$

c. $5 - 4 = \boxed{}$

d. $7 - 2 = \boxed{}$

e. $2 + 8 = \boxed{}$

f. $1 + 9 = \boxed{}$

g. $6 + 1 = \boxed{}$

h. $2 + 10 = \boxed{}$

Part 2

a. $8 - 2 = \boxed{}$

b. $12 - 2 = \boxed{}$

c. $6 - 2 = \boxed{}$

d. $10 - 2 = \boxed{}$

e. $4 - 2 = \boxed{}$

Part 3

a.
You have 16 birds.
Then you find 12 more birds. How many birds do you end up with?

b.
You have 26 cups.
You buy 21 more cups.
How many cups do you end up with?

c.
You have 28 cats.
You find 41 more cats.
How many cats do you end up with?

d.
You have 22 shoes.
You buy 64 more shoes.
How many shoes do you end up with?

Part 4

a. $9 - 1 = \boxed{}$

b. $9 - 2 = \boxed{}$

c. $9 + 2 = \boxed{}$

d. $4 - 1 = \boxed{}$

e. $6 + 2 = \boxed{}$

f. $11 - 2 = \boxed{}$

Part 5

a. $6 - 4 =$ ☐

b. $6 - 5 =$ ☐

c. $6 - 6 =$ ☐

d. $9 - 8 =$ ☐

e. $8 - 7 =$ ☐

f. $8 - 8 =$ ☐

g. $10 - 10 =$ ☐

h. $11 - 10 =$ ☐

i. $11 - 11 =$ ☐

Part 6

	First day	Second day	Third day
Train X	600	531	580
Train Y	450	605	575
Train Z	280	725	451

a. Train X on the second day? _____

b. Train X on the third day? _____

c. Train Z on the first day? _____

d. Train Y on the second day? _____

Part 7

a. $10 - 8 =$ ☐

b. $8 - 6 =$ ☐

c. $6 - 4 =$ ☐

d. $12 - 10 =$ ☐

e. $6 - 2 =$ ☐

f. $8 - 2 =$ ☐

g. $10 - 2 =$ ☐

h. $4 - 2 =$ ☐

Part 8

a.
```
+
 7 1
```

b.
```
+
 1 3
```

c.
```
+
 2 6
```

d.
```
+
 4 9
```

Part 9

a.
```
  3 6
+ 1 2
```

b.
```
  2 0
+ 6 9
```

c.
```
  6 8
+ 2 1
```

d.
```
  2 4
+ 4 2
```

Lesson 48

Part 1

a. $4 - 2 = \boxed{}$ d. $8 - 1 = \boxed{}$ g. $5 - 4 = \boxed{}$

b. $4 - 3 = \boxed{}$ e. $8 - 7 = \boxed{}$ h. $6 - 5 = \boxed{}$

c. $4 - 4 = \boxed{}$ f. $8 - 8 = \boxed{}$ i. $6 - 6 = \boxed{}$

Part 2

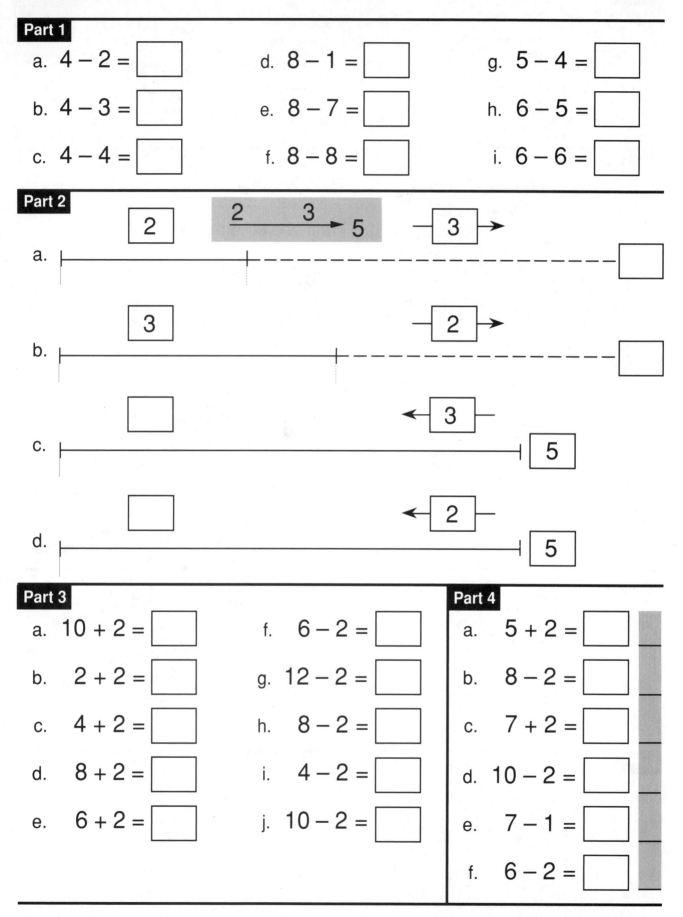

Part 3

a. $10 + 2 = \boxed{}$ f. $6 - 2 = \boxed{}$

b. $2 + 2 = \boxed{}$ g. $12 - 2 = \boxed{}$

c. $4 + 2 = \boxed{}$ h. $8 - 2 = \boxed{}$

d. $8 + 2 = \boxed{}$ i. $4 - 2 = \boxed{}$

e. $6 + 2 = \boxed{}$ j. $10 - 2 = \boxed{}$

Part 4

a. $5 + 2 = \boxed{}$

b. $8 - 2 = \boxed{}$

c. $7 + 2 = \boxed{}$

d. $10 - 2 = \boxed{}$

e. $7 - 1 = \boxed{}$

f. $6 - 2 = \boxed{}$

Part 5

a.
Carlos has 32 pens.
Then he buys 16 more pens.
How many pens does he end up with?

c.
Carlos has 44 books.
He buys 21 more books.
How many books does he end up with?

b.
Carlos has 12 hats.
He makes 26 more hats.
How many hats does he end up with?

d.
Carlos has 61 cups.
He finds 25 more cups.
How many cups does he end up with?

Part 6

a.
$$\begin{array}{r} 6 \\ -\ 4 \\ \hline \end{array}$$
b.
$$\begin{array}{r} 10 \\ -\ 2 \\ \hline \end{array}$$
c.
$$\begin{array}{r} 12 \\ -\ 2 \\ \hline \end{array}$$
d.
$$\begin{array}{r} 8 \\ -\ 2 \\ \hline \end{array}$$
e.
$$\begin{array}{r} 8 \\ -\ 6 \\ \hline \end{array}$$
f.
$$\begin{array}{r} 4 \\ -\ 2 \\ \hline \end{array}$$
g.
$$\begin{array}{r} 10 \\ -\ 8 \\ \hline \end{array}$$

Part 7

a.
$$\begin{array}{r} 56 \\ +\ 12 \\ \hline \end{array}$$
b.
$$\begin{array}{r} 80 \\ +\ 15 \\ \hline \end{array}$$

Part 8

a. ☐ cents

b. ☐ cents

c. ☐ cents

Lesson 49

Part 1

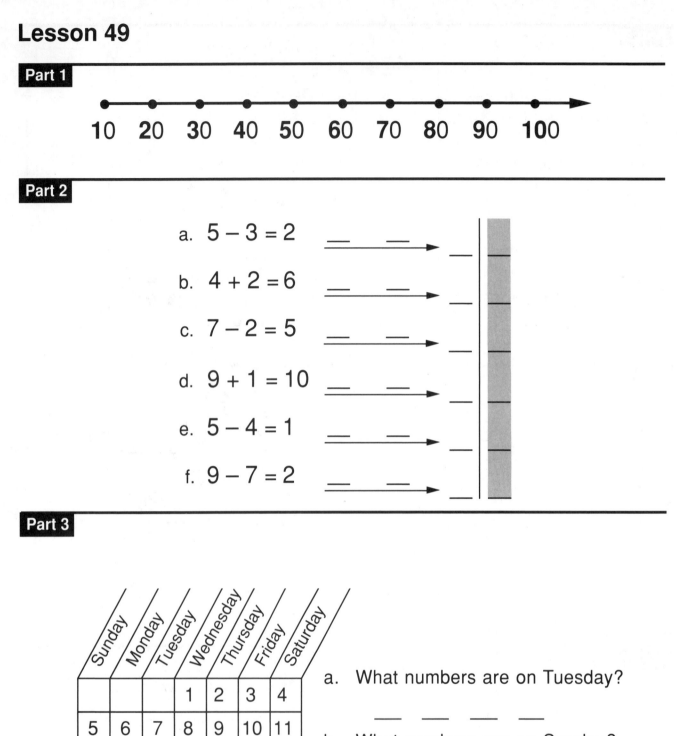

10　20　30　40　50　60　70　80　90　100

Part 2

a. $5 - 3 = 2$

b. $4 + 2 = 6$

c. $7 - 2 = 5$

d. $9 + 1 = 10$

e. $5 - 4 = 1$

f. $9 - 7 = 2$

Part 3

Sunday	Monday	Tuesday	Wednesday	Thursday	Friday	Saturday
			1	2	3	4
5	6	7	8	9	10	11
12	13	14	15	16	17	18
19	20	21	22	23	24	25
26	27	28	29	30	31	

a. What numbers are on Tuesday?

___ ___ ___ ___

b. What numbers are on Sunday?

___ ___ ___ ___

c. What numbers are on Saturday?

___ ___ ___ ___

Part 4

a. $5 - 1 =$ ☐   e. $7 - 6 =$ ☐   i. $7 - 1 =$ ☐

b. $8 + 2 =$ ☐   f. $1 + 6 =$ ☐   j. $10 + 2 =$ ☐

c. $11 - 1 =$ ☐   g. $5 - 4 =$ ☐   k. $3 - 1 =$ ☐

d. $8 + 1 =$ ☐   h. $2 + 6 =$ ☐   l. $3 + 1 =$ ☐

Part 5

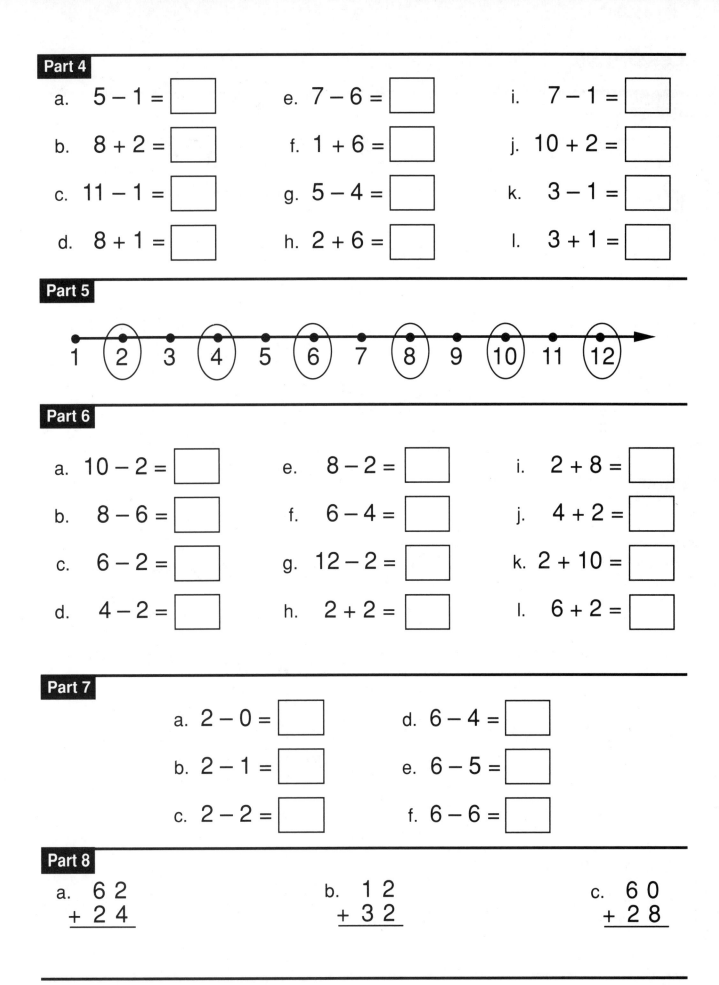

Part 6

a. $10 - 2 =$ ☐   e. $8 - 2 =$ ☐   i. $2 + 8 =$ ☐

b. $8 - 6 =$ ☐   f. $6 - 4 =$ ☐   j. $4 + 2 =$ ☐

c. $6 - 2 =$ ☐   g. $12 - 2 =$ ☐   k. $2 + 10 =$ ☐

d. $4 - 2 =$ ☐   h. $2 + 2 =$ ☐   l. $6 + 2 =$ ☐

Part 7

a. $2 - 0 =$ ☐   d. $6 - 4 =$ ☐

b. $2 - 1 =$ ☐   e. $6 - 5 =$ ☐

c. $2 - 2 =$ ☐   f. $6 - 6 =$ ☐

Part 8

a. $\begin{array}{r} 62 \\ + 24 \\ \hline \end{array}$ b. $\begin{array}{r} 12 \\ + 32 \\ \hline \end{array}$ c. $\begin{array}{r} 60 \\ + 28 \\ \hline \end{array}$

109

Lesson 50

Part 1

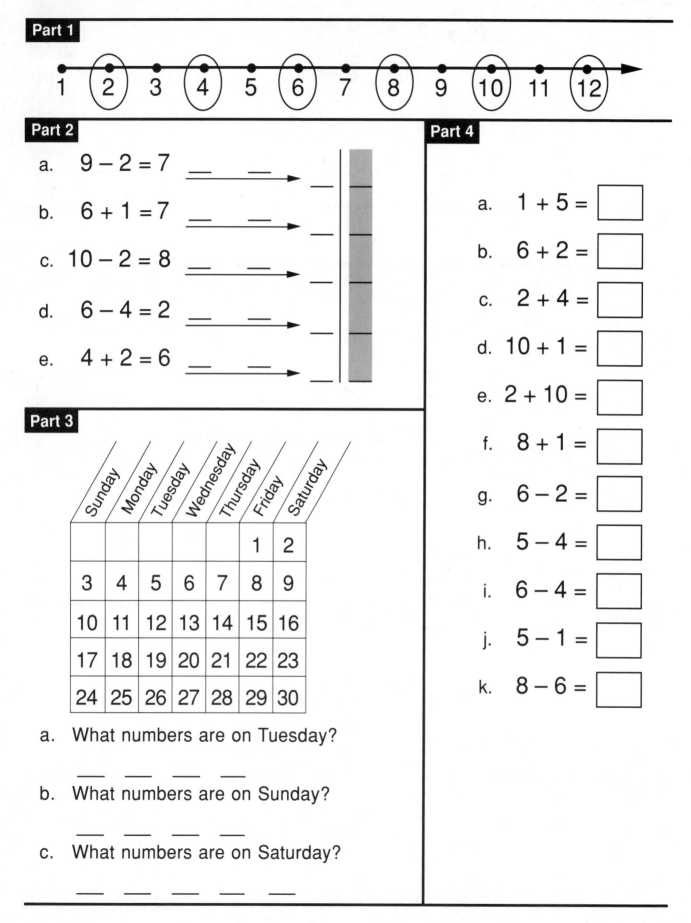

Part 2

a. $9 - 2 = 7$ ___ ___

b. $6 + 1 = 7$ ___ ___

c. $10 - 2 = 8$ ___ ___

d. $6 - 4 = 2$ ___ ___

e. $4 + 2 = 6$ ___ ___

Part 3

Sunday	Monday	Tuesday	Wednesday	Thursday	Friday	Saturday
					1	2
3	4	5	6	7	8	9
10	11	12	13	14	15	16
17	18	19	20	21	22	23
24	25	26	27	28	29	30

a. What numbers are on Tuesday?

___ ___ ___ ___

b. What numbers are on Sunday?

___ ___ ___ ___

c. What numbers are on Saturday?

___ ___ ___ ___ ___

Part 4

a. $1 + 5 =$ ☐

b. $6 + 2 =$ ☐

c. $2 + 4 =$ ☐

d. $10 + 1 =$ ☐

e. $2 + 10 =$ ☐

f. $8 + 1 =$ ☐

g. $6 - 2 =$ ☐

h. $5 - 4 =$ ☐

i. $6 - 4 =$ ☐

j. $5 - 1 =$ ☐

k. $8 - 6 =$ ☐

10 20 30 40 50 60 70 80 90 100

Part 6

A	
B	

a. $6 + 1 = \boxed{}$

b. $10 - 1 = \boxed{}$

c. $6 + 2 = \boxed{}$

d. $8 - 7 = \boxed{}$

e. $2 + 8 = \boxed{}$

f. $10 + 2 = \boxed{}$

g. $5 - 1 = \boxed{}$

h. $2 + 6 = \boxed{}$

i. $3 - 2 = \boxed{}$

j. $4 + 2 = \boxed{}$

k. $1 + 7 = \boxed{}$

l. $9 - 1 = \boxed{}$

m. $11 - 10 = \boxed{}$

Part 7

a.
You have 62 pounds.
You get 22 more pounds.
How many pounds do you end up with?

b.
Rita has 14 cats.
She buys 21 more cats.
How many cats does she end up with?

Part 8

a. $2 \longrightarrow 8$

b. $1 \longrightarrow 8$

c. $2 \longrightarrow 10$

d. $1 \longrightarrow 10$

e. $1 \longrightarrow 6$

f. $2 \longrightarrow 6$

Part 9

a. $\begin{array}{r} 7 \\ -7 \\ \hline \end{array}$
b. $\begin{array}{r} 7 \\ -0 \\ \hline \end{array}$
c. $\begin{array}{r} 7 \\ -1 \\ \hline \end{array}$
d. $\begin{array}{r} 6 \\ -1 \\ \hline \end{array}$
e. $\begin{array}{r} 6 \\ -2 \\ \hline \end{array}$
f. $\begin{array}{r} 6 \\ -0 \\ \hline \end{array}$
g. $\begin{array}{r} 4 \\ -4 \\ \hline \end{array}$
h. $\begin{array}{r} 4 \\ -3 \\ \hline \end{array}$
i. $\begin{array}{r} 4 \\ -2 \\ \hline \end{array}$

Test Lesson 5

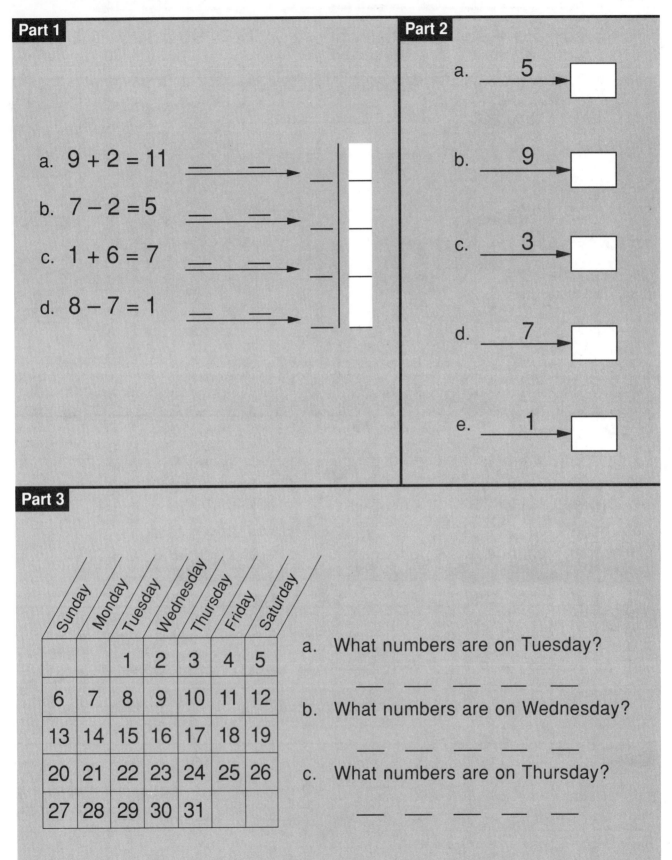

Part 1

a. 9 + 2 = 11 ___ ___ ⟶ ___

b. 7 − 2 = 5 ___ ___ ⟶ ___

c. 1 + 6 = 7 ___ ___ ⟶ ___

d. 8 − 7 = 1 ___ ___ ⟶ ___

Part 2

a. ⟶ 5 ▢

b. ⟶ 9 ▢

c. ⟶ 3 ▢

d. ⟶ 7 ▢

e. ⟶ 1 ▢

Part 3

Sunday	Monday	Tuesday	Wednesday	Thursday	Friday	Saturday
		1	2	3	4	5
6	7	8	9	10	11	12
13	14	15	16	17	18	19
20	21	22	23	24	25	26
27	28	29	30	31		

a. What numbers are on Tuesday?

___ ___ ___ ___ ___

b. What numbers are on Wednesday?

___ ___ ___ ___ ___

c. What numbers are on Thursday?

___ ___ ___ ___ ___

Test 5

Part 1

a. $8 - 1 =$ ☐   g. $2 - 1 =$ ☐

b. $9 + 1 =$ ☐   h. $2 + 10 =$ ☐

c. $6 + 2 =$ ☐   i. $7 - 1 =$ ☐

d. $11 - 10 =$ ☐   j. $9 - 8 =$ ☐

e. $2 + 1 =$ ☐   k. $2 + 4 =$ ☐

f. $1 + 7 =$ ☐

Part 2

a.

b.

c.

d.

e.

Part 3 Write the number problems and the answers.

a.
You have 16 beads.
You buy 22 more beads.
How many beads do you end up with?

b.
You have 72 cups.
You make 14 more cups.
How many cups do you end up with?

Part 4 Write the answers.

5 2 6

a. How many tens? ☐

b. How many hundreds? ☐

Part 5

	First day	Second day	Third day
Train X	600	250	480
Train Y	220	251	326
Train Z	310	252	311

a. Train Z on the first day? _____

b. Train Y on the third day? _____

Part 6 Write all the numbers for counting by 5.

___ ___ ___ ___ ___ ___ ___ ___

Write all the numbers for counting by 2.

___ ___ ___ ___ ___ ___ ___ ___

113

Extra Practice/Test 5

Part 1

a. $10 + 2 = \boxed{}$

b. $2 + 6 = \boxed{}$

c. $1 + 4 = \boxed{}$

d. $2 + 8 = \boxed{}$

e. $9 - 1 = \boxed{}$

f. $4 - 3 = \boxed{}$

g. $8 - 7 = \boxed{}$

h. $10 - 1 = \boxed{}$

Part 2

a.

b.

c.

d.

e.

Part 3

a.
You have 16 birds.
You find 12 more birds.
How many birds do you
end up with?

b.
You have 26 cups.
You buy 21 more cups.
How many cups do you
end up with?

c.
You have 28 cats.
You find 41 more cats.
How many cats do
you end up with?

d.
You have 22 shoes.
You buy 64 more shoes.
How many shoes do
you end up with?

Part 4

a. 5 6 3   How many tens? $\boxed{}$ How many hundreds? $\boxed{}$

b. 3 9 0   How many hundreds? $\boxed{}$ How many ones? $\boxed{}$

c. 9 0 3   How many ones? $\boxed{}$ How many tens? $\boxed{}$

Part 5

	5 years	10 years	15 years
Pine tree	8	12	19
Oak tree	6	11	16
Elm tree	7	14	18

a. Oak tree at 15 years? _____

b. Elm tree at 5 years? _____

c. Oak tree at 5 years? _____

d. Pine tree at 10 years? _____

Lesson 51

Part 1

a. $3 - 1 = \boxed{}$

b. $8 + 2 = \boxed{}$

c. $11 - 10 = \boxed{}$

d. $2 + 10 = \boxed{}$

e. $4 + 2 = \boxed{}$

f. $7 - 1 = \boxed{}$

g. $7 - 0 = \boxed{}$

h. $6 + 1 = \boxed{}$

i. $6 - 5 = \boxed{}$

j. $2 + 6 = \boxed{}$

k. $2 - 2 = \boxed{}$

l. $9 - 9 = \boxed{}$

m. $9 - 8 = \boxed{}$

Part 2

a. $7 \longrightarrow \boxed{}$

b. $3 \longrightarrow \boxed{}$

c. $9 \longrightarrow \boxed{}$

d. $5 \longrightarrow \boxed{}$

e. $1 \longrightarrow \boxed{}$

Part 3

a. $2 \qquad 7 \longrightarrow \underline{}$

b. $2 \qquad 3 \longrightarrow \underline{}$

c. $2 \qquad 9 \longrightarrow \underline{}$

d. $2 \qquad 5 \longrightarrow \underline{}$

Part 4

Sunday	Monday	Tuesday	Wednesday	Thursday	Friday	Saturday
					1	2
3	4	5	6	7	8	9
10	11	12	13	14	15	16
17	18	19	20	21	22	23
24	25	26	27	28	29	30

a. Write all the numbers that are on Friday.

____ ____ ____ ____ ____

b. What's the number for the first Sunday? ____

c. What's the number for the third Tuesday? ____

d. What's the number for the fourth Saturday? ____

a. $8 - 6 =$ ☐   e. $4 - 2 =$ ☐   i. $6 - 2 =$ ☐

b. $2 + 10 =$ ☐   f. $8 + 2 =$ ☐   j. $6 - 4 =$ ☐

c. $10 - 8 =$ ☐   g. $2 + 4 =$ ☐   k. $2 + 8 =$ ☐

d. $6 + 2 =$ ☐   h. $8 - 2 =$ ☐   l. $10 - 2 =$ ☐

Part 6

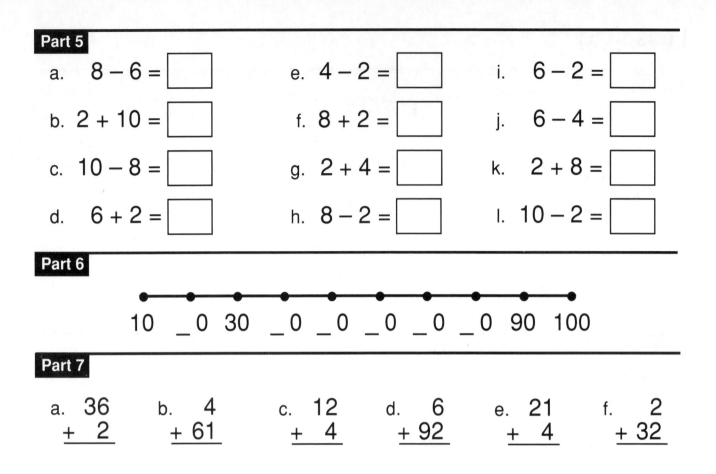

10   _0 30   _0 _0 _0 _0 _0 90 100

Part 7

a. $\begin{array}{r} 36 \\ +\ 2 \\ \hline \end{array}$ b. $\begin{array}{r} 4 \\ +61 \\ \hline \end{array}$ c. $\begin{array}{r} 12 \\ +\ 4 \\ \hline \end{array}$ d. $\begin{array}{r} 6 \\ +92 \\ \hline \end{array}$ e. $\begin{array}{r} 21 \\ +\ 4 \\ \hline \end{array}$ f. $\begin{array}{r} 2 \\ +32 \\ \hline \end{array}$

Part 8

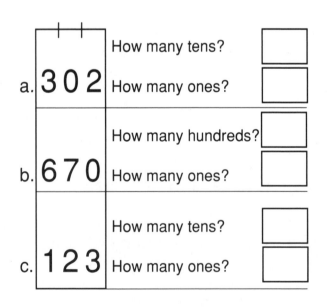

a. **302** How many tens? ☐
        How many ones? ☐

b. **670** How many hundreds? ☐
        How many ones? ☐

c. **123** How many tens? ☐
        How many ones? ☐

Lesson 52

Part 1

10 _ _0 _ _0 _ _0 50 _ _0 _ _0 80 _ _0 100

Part 2

a. $\dfrac{2 \qquad 7}{} \rightarrow$ __

b. $\dfrac{2 \qquad 3}{} \rightarrow$ __

c. $\dfrac{2 \qquad 9}{} \rightarrow$ __

d. $\dfrac{2 \qquad 5}{} \rightarrow$ __

Part 3

a. 8 − 2 = ☐

b. 2 + 10 = ☐

c. 6 − 4 = ☐

d. 8 + 2 = ☐

e. 12 − 2 = ☐

f. 4 + 2 = ☐

g. 2 + 6 = ☐

h. 12 − 10 = ☐

i. 6 − 2 = ☐

j. 10 − 8 = ☐

Part 4

Sunday	Monday	Tuesday	Wednesday	Thursday	Friday	Saturday
		1	2	3	4	5
6	7	8	9	10	11	12
13	14	15	16	17	18	19
20	21	22	23	24	25	26
27	28	29	30	31		

a. Write all the numbers that are on Tuesday.

____ ____ ____ ____ ____

b. What's the number for the second Sunday? ____

c. What's the number for the fourth Saturday? ____

d. What's the number for the first Monday? ____

117

a. 412
+206

b. 204
+192

c. 195
+300

d. 241
+627

a. 26 + 1 = ☐

c. 24 + 1 = ☐

e. 60 + 1 = ☐

b. 1 + 98 = ☐

d. 1 + 40 = ☐

A	
B	

a. 5
+ 1

b. 8
− 8

c. 2
+ 8

d. 9
− 1

e. 6
− 5

f. 6
+ 2

g. 3
− 1

h. 1
+ 4

i. 6
+ 0

j. 6
− 0

k. 9
+ 1

l. 11
− 10

m. 3
− 0

n. 8
+ 2

o. 8
− 1

p. 1
+ 7

q. 5
− 5

r. 4
− 3

s. 2
− 1

t. 4
+ 2

a. 2 ——— 5 ——→ 7

b. 2 ——— 7 ——→ 9

Write two
subtraction { _____
facts.   _____

Write two
subtraction { _____
facts.   _____

Lesson 53

Part 1

_0 _0 _0 _0 _0 _0 _0 _0 _0 __0

Part 2

a. 2   5   → __

b. 2   3   → __

c. 2   9   → __

d. 2   7   → __

Part 3

a. $7 + 2 = \boxed{}$　　f. $1 + 2 = \boxed{}$

b. $2 + 3 = \boxed{}$　　g. $2 + 5 = \boxed{}$

c. $9 + 2 = \boxed{}$　　h. $3 + 2 = \boxed{}$

d. $2 + 7 = \boxed{}$　　i. $2 + 1 = \boxed{}$

e. $2 + 9 = \boxed{}$　　j. $5 + 2 = \boxed{}$

Part 4

Sunday	Monday	Tuesday	Wednesday	Thursday	Friday	Saturday
			1	2	3	4
5	6	7	8	9	10	11
12	13	14	15	16	17	18
19	20	21	22	23	24	25
26	27	28	29	30		

a. What number is 2 weeks after 15? ____

b. What number is 3 weeks after 7? ____

c. What number is 1 week after 14? ____

d. What number is 3 weeks after 2? ____

Part 5

a. 10 − 2 = ☐

b. 10 + 2 = ☐

c. 6 − 2 = ☐

d. 8 − 6 = ☐

e. 4 − 2 = ☐

f. 2 + 4 = ☐

g. 6 − 4 = ☐

h. 8 − 2 = ☐

i. 10 − 8 = ☐

j. 4 + 2 = ☐

k. 2 + 6 = ☐

l. 8 + 2 = ☐

Part 6

a.
$$
\begin{array}{r} 601 \\ +257 \\ \hline \end{array}
$$

b.
$$
\begin{array}{r} 280 \\ +612 \\ \hline \end{array}
$$

c.
$$
\begin{array}{r} 210 \\ +210 \\ \hline \end{array}
$$

d.
$$
\begin{array}{r} 640 \\ +126 \\ \hline \end{array}
$$

Part 7

a. 1 + 56 = ☐

b. 24 + 1 = ☐

c. 48 + 1 = ☐

d. 87 + 1 = ☐

e. 1 + 96 = ☐

Part 8

A	
B	

a.
$$
\begin{array}{r} 6 \\ -2 \\ \hline \end{array}
$$

b.
$$
\begin{array}{r} 7 \\ +0 \\ \hline \end{array}
$$

c.
$$
\begin{array}{r} 7 \\ +1 \\ \hline \end{array}
$$

d.
$$
\begin{array}{r} 10 \\ -8 \\ \hline \end{array}
$$

e.
$$
\begin{array}{r} 4 \\ -2 \\ \hline \end{array}
$$

f.
$$
\begin{array}{r} 0 \\ +8 \\ \hline \end{array}
$$

g.
$$
\begin{array}{r} 2 \\ +8 \\ \hline \end{array}
$$

h.
$$
\begin{array}{r} 6 \\ -4 \\ \hline \end{array}
$$

i.
$$
\begin{array}{r} 7 \\ -6 \\ \hline \end{array}
$$

j.
$$
\begin{array}{r} 2 \\ +4 \\ \hline \end{array}
$$

k.
$$
\begin{array}{r} 10 \\ -8 \\ \hline \end{array}
$$

l.
$$
\begin{array}{r} 7 \\ -7 \\ \hline \end{array}
$$

m.
$$
\begin{array}{r} 1 \\ +8 \\ \hline \end{array}
$$

n.
$$
\begin{array}{r} 5 \\ +1 \\ \hline \end{array}
$$

o.
$$
\begin{array}{r} 2 \\ +10 \\ \hline \end{array}
$$

p.
$$
\begin{array}{r} 8 \\ -2 \\ \hline \end{array}
$$

q.
$$
\begin{array}{r} 9 \\ -0 \\ \hline \end{array}
$$

r.
$$
\begin{array}{r} 8 \\ +2 \\ \hline \end{array}
$$

s.
$$
\begin{array}{r} 1 \\ +4 \\ \hline \end{array}
$$

t.
$$
\begin{array}{r} 2 \\ +2 \\ \hline \end{array}
$$

Lesson 54

Part 1

a. $3 + 2 = \boxed{}$

b. $2 + 4 = \boxed{}$

c. $2 + 9 = \boxed{}$

d. $5 + 2 = \boxed{}$

e. $7 + 2 = \boxed{}$

f. $2 + 3 = \boxed{}$

g. $2 + 6 = \boxed{}$

h. $2 + 7 = \boxed{}$

i. $8 + 2 = \boxed{}$

j. $9 + 2 = \boxed{}$

k. $10 + 2 = \boxed{}$

l. $2 + 5 = \boxed{}$

Part 2

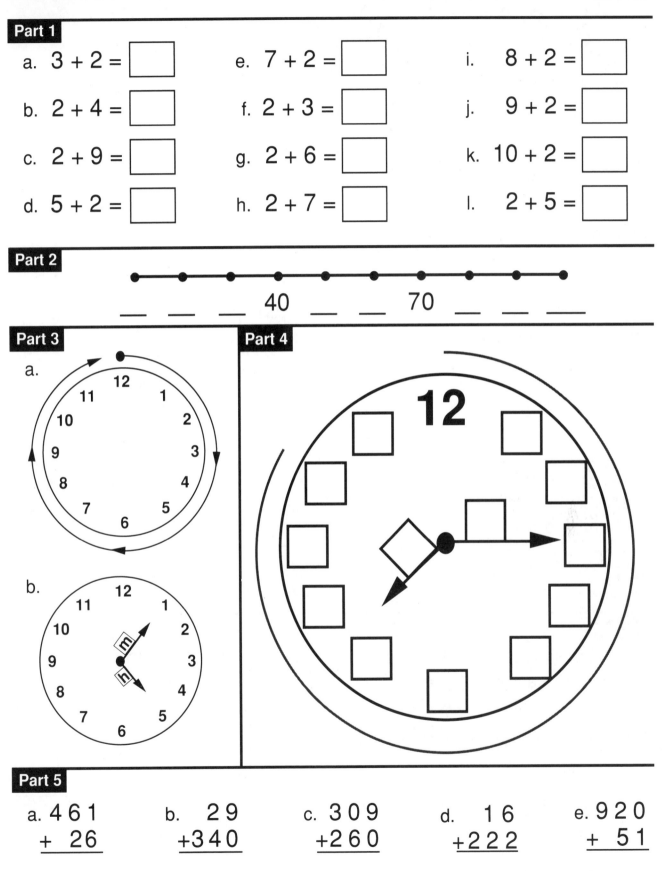

___ ___ ___ 40 ___ ___ 70 ___ ___ ___

Part 3

a.

b.

Part 4

12

Part 5

a.
$$\begin{array}{r} 461 \\ +26 \\ \hline \end{array}$$

b.
$$\begin{array}{r} 29 \\ +340 \\ \hline \end{array}$$

c.
$$\begin{array}{r} 309 \\ +260 \\ \hline \end{array}$$

d.
$$\begin{array}{r} 16 \\ +222 \\ \hline \end{array}$$

e.
$$\begin{array}{r} 920 \\ +51 \\ \hline \end{array}$$

Part 6

	Sunday	Monday	Tuesday	Wednesday	Thursday	Friday	Saturday
		1	2	3	4	5	6
	7	8	9	10	11	12	13
	14	15	16	17	18	19	20
	21	22	23	24	25	26	27
	28	29	30	31			

a. What number is 4 days after 3? _____

b. What number is 4 weeks after 3? _____

c. What number is 5 days after 9? _____

d. What number is 1 week after 17? _____

e. What number is 5 days after 17? _____

Part 7

a. $10 - 2 =$ ☐

b. $4 - 4 =$ ☐

c. $4 + 2 =$ ☐

d. $6 - 4 =$ ☐

e. $2 + 6 =$ ☐

f. $10 - 8 =$ ☐

g. $10 - 9 =$ ☐

h. $10 - 10 =$ ☐

i. $8 - 6 =$ ☐

j. $4 - 2 =$ ☐

k. $4 - 1 =$ ☐

l. $4 - 0 =$ ☐

m. $6 - 2 =$ ☐

n. $2 + 10 =$ ☐

o. $12 - 2 =$ ☐

p. $7 - 7 =$ ☐

Part 8

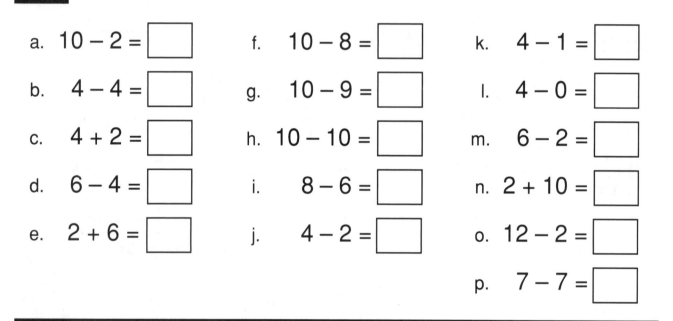

a. $\dfrac{2 \qquad 7}{\qquad} \to 9$

Write two subtraction facts. { _____

_____

b. $\dfrac{2 \qquad 3}{\qquad} \to 5$

Write two subtraction facts. { _____

_____

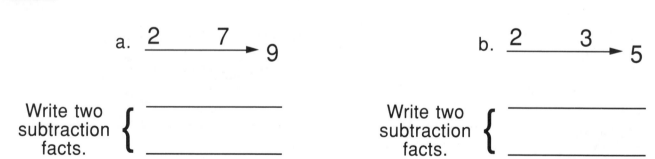

Lesson 55

Part 1

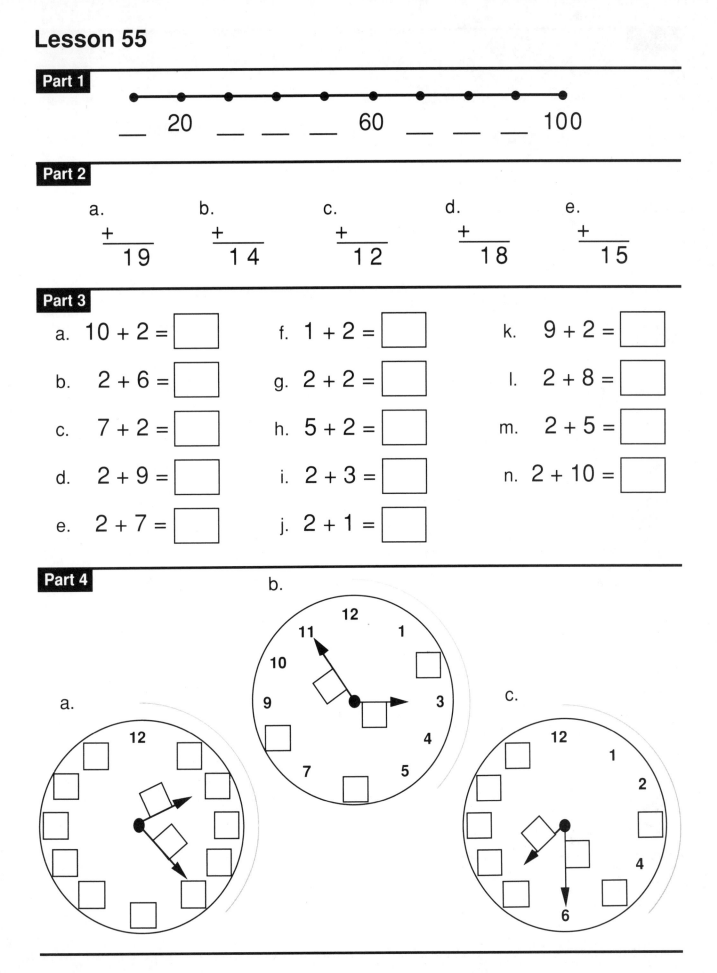

___ 20 ___ ___ ___ 60 ___ ___ ___ 100

Part 2

a.
$$+\atop 19$$

b.
$$+\atop 14$$

c.
$$+\atop 12$$

d.
$$+\atop 18$$

e.
$$+\atop 15$$

Part 3

a. 10 + 2 = ☐

b. 2 + 6 = ☐

c. 7 + 2 = ☐

d. 2 + 9 = ☐

e. 2 + 7 = ☐

f. 1 + 2 = ☐

g. 2 + 2 = ☐

h. 5 + 2 = ☐

i. 2 + 3 = ☐

j. 2 + 1 = ☐

k. 9 + 2 = ☐

l. 2 + 8 = ☐

m. 2 + 5 = ☐

n. 2 + 10 = ☐

Part 4

a.

b.

c.

Part 5

Sunday	Monday	Tuesday	Wednesday	Thursday	Friday	Saturday
			1	2	3	4
5	6	7	8	9	10	11
12	13	14	15	16	17	18
19	20	21	22	23	24	25
26	27	28	29	30	31	

a. What number is 4 days after 8? ____

b. What number is 3 weeks after 6? ____

c. What number is 5 days after 12? ____

d. What number is 2 weeks after 3? ____

e. What number is 2 weeks after 11? ____

Part 6

a. $\begin{array}{r} 30 \\ +827 \\ \hline \end{array}$

b. $\begin{array}{r} 73 \\ +222 \\ \hline \end{array}$

c. $\begin{array}{r} 258 \\ +720 \\ \hline \end{array}$

d. $\begin{array}{r} 52 \\ +615 \\ \hline \end{array}$

e. $\begin{array}{r} 362 \\ +226 \\ \hline \end{array}$

Part 7

a. $\begin{array}{r} 6 \\ -4 \\ \hline \end{array}$

b. $\begin{array}{r} 6 \\ -5 \\ \hline \end{array}$

c. $\begin{array}{r} 6 \\ -6 \\ \hline \end{array}$

d. $\begin{array}{r} 6 \\ -0 \\ \hline \end{array}$

e. $\begin{array}{r} 6 \\ -1 \\ \hline \end{array}$

f. $\begin{array}{r} 6 \\ -2 \\ \hline \end{array}$

g. $\begin{array}{r} 8 \\ -2 \\ \hline \end{array}$

h. $\begin{array}{r} 4 \\ -2 \\ \hline \end{array}$

i. $\begin{array}{r} 4 \\ -3 \\ \hline \end{array}$

j. $\begin{array}{r} 4 \\ -4 \\ \hline \end{array}$

k. $\begin{array}{r} 4 \\ -1 \\ \hline \end{array}$

l. $\begin{array}{r} 4 \\ -0 \\ \hline \end{array}$

m. $\begin{array}{r} 10 \\ -10 \\ \hline \end{array}$

n. $\begin{array}{r} 10 \\ -9 \\ \hline \end{array}$

o. $\begin{array}{r} 10 \\ -8 \\ \hline \end{array}$

p. $\begin{array}{r} 10 \\ -2 \\ \hline \end{array}$

q. $\begin{array}{r} 10 \\ -1 \\ \hline \end{array}$

r. $\begin{array}{r} 10 \\ -0 \\ \hline \end{array}$

Lesson 56

Part 1

1　②　3　④　5　⑥　7　⑧　9　⑩　11　⑫　→

Part 2

a. 2 [ ] → 7

b. 2 [ ] → 11

c. 2 [ ] → 5

d. 2 [ ] → 9

Part 3

a.
```
  +
 1 2
```

b.
```
  +
 1 6
```

c.
```
  +
 1 3
```

d.
```
  +
 1 7
```

e.
```
  +
 1 1
```

Part 4

a. 3　10 → [ ]

b. 5　10 → [ ]

c. 10　10 → [ ]

d. 7　10 → [ ]

e. 2　10 → [ ]

f. 8　10 → [ ]

Part 5

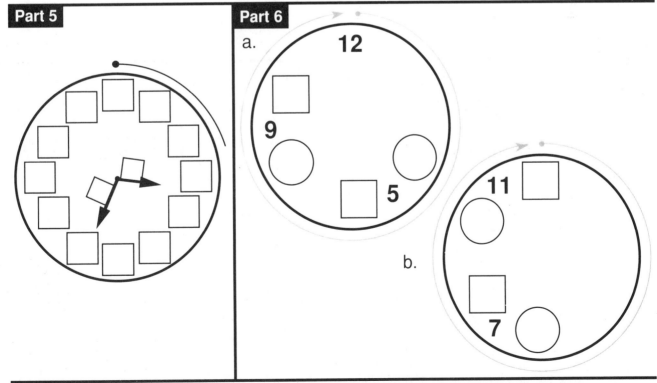

Part 6

a.

b.

125

Sunday	Monday	Tuesday	Wednesday	Thursday	Friday	Saturday
		1	2	3	4	5
6	7	8	9	10	11	12
13	14	15	16	17	18	19
20	21	22	23	24	25	26
27	28	29	30	31		

a. What number is 4 days after 3? ____

b. What number is 4 weeks after 3? ____

c. What number is 5 days after 9? ____

d. What number is 3 weeks after 10? ____

e. What number is 3 days after 18? ____

Part 8

a. 6   b. 8   c. 8   d. 8   e. 8   f. 8
  -2 -2 -1 -0 -8 -7

g. 8   h.10   i. 6   j. 4   k. 4
  -6 -2 -4 -2 -1

Part 9

a. Jan has 6 dogs.
    She sells 4 dogs.
    How many dogs does
    she end up with?

b. Jan has 8 shoes.
    She loses 6 shoes.
    How many shoes does
    she end up with?

Lesson 57

Part 1

a. 10   10 ➡ ☐   b. 6   10 ➡ ☐   c. 2   10 ➡ ☐

d. 5   10 ➡ ☐   e. 3   10 ➡ ☐   f. 7   10 ➡ ☐

Part 2

a. 2   b. 1   c. 3   d. 1   e. 2   f. 1
    7   2   2   6   5   3
 + 1   + 1   + 2   + 2   + 2   + 2

Part 3

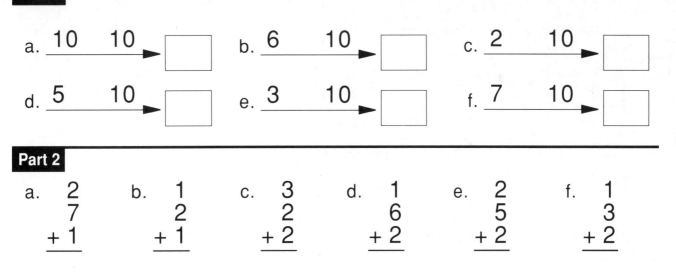

Part 4

a. one hundred
    +
   no tens
    +
   three ones

b. seven hundreds
    +
   five tens
    +
   no ones

Part 5

Fred has 6 coins.
He loses 2 coins.
How many coins does
he end up with?

Part 6   Write all the numbers for counting by 5.

____ ____ ____ ____ ____ ____ ____ ____ ____ ____

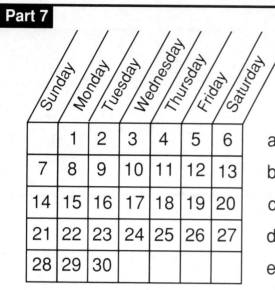

	Sunday	Monday	Tuesday	Wednesday	Thursday	Friday	Saturday
		1	2	3	4	5	6
	7	8	9	10	11	12	13
	14	15	16	17	18	19	20
	21	22	23	24	25	26	27
	28	29	30				

a. What number is 6 days after 4? ____

b. What number is 2 weeks after 5? ____

c. What number is 4 days after 13? ____

d. What number is 3 weeks after 9? ____

e. What number is 3 days after 9? ____

Part 8

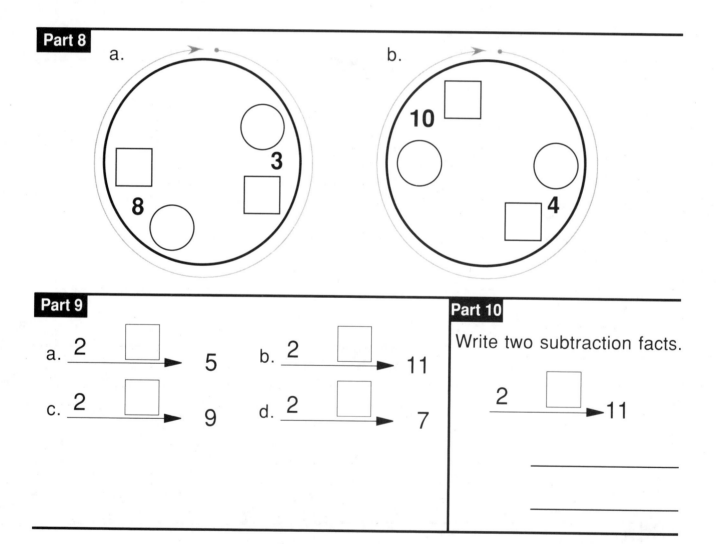

a.

b.

Part 9

a. 2 ⬜ → 5

b. 2 ⬜ → 11

c. 2 ⬜ → 9

d. 2 ⬜ → 7

Part 10

Write two subtraction facts.

2 ⬜ → 11

_____

_____

Lesson 58

a. $\dfrac{4 \qquad 10}{\qquad\longrightarrow}$ __ b. $\dfrac{1 \qquad 10}{\qquad\longrightarrow}$ __ c. $\dfrac{8 \qquad 10}{\qquad\longrightarrow}$ __

d. $\dfrac{2 \qquad 10}{\qquad\longrightarrow}$ __ e. $\dfrac{10 \qquad 10}{\qquad\longrightarrow}$ __ f. $\dfrac{5 \qquad 10}{\qquad\longrightarrow}$ __

Part 2

a. $11 - 2 =$ ☐ __ b. $5 - 2 =$ ☐ __ c. $8 - 2 =$ ☐ __

d. $7 - 2 =$ ☐ __ e. $6 - 2 =$ ☐ __ f. $9 - 2 =$ ☐ __

Part 3

a. $\begin{array}{r} 1 \\ 1 \\ +\ 5 \\ \hline \end{array}$ b. $\begin{array}{r} 2 \\ 7 \\ +\ 1 \\ \hline \end{array}$ c. $\begin{array}{r} 9 \\ 2 \\ +\ 1 \\ \hline \end{array}$ d. $\begin{array}{r} 10 \\ 2 \\ +\ 1 \\ \hline \end{array}$ e. $\begin{array}{r} 2 \\ 6 \\ +\ 2 \\ \hline \end{array}$ f. $\begin{array}{r} 3 \\ 2 \\ +\ 2 \\ \hline \end{array}$

Part 4

1   2   3   4

Part 5

	Sunday	Monday	Tuesday	Wednesday	Thursday	Friday	Saturday
		1	2	3	4	5	6
	7	8	9	10	11	12	13
	14	15	16	17	18	19	20
	21	22	23	24	25	26	27
	28	29	30				

a. What number is 4 days after 5? ____

b. What number is 7 days after 11? ____

c. What number is 7 days after 19? ____

d. What number is 1 week after 19? ____

Part 6

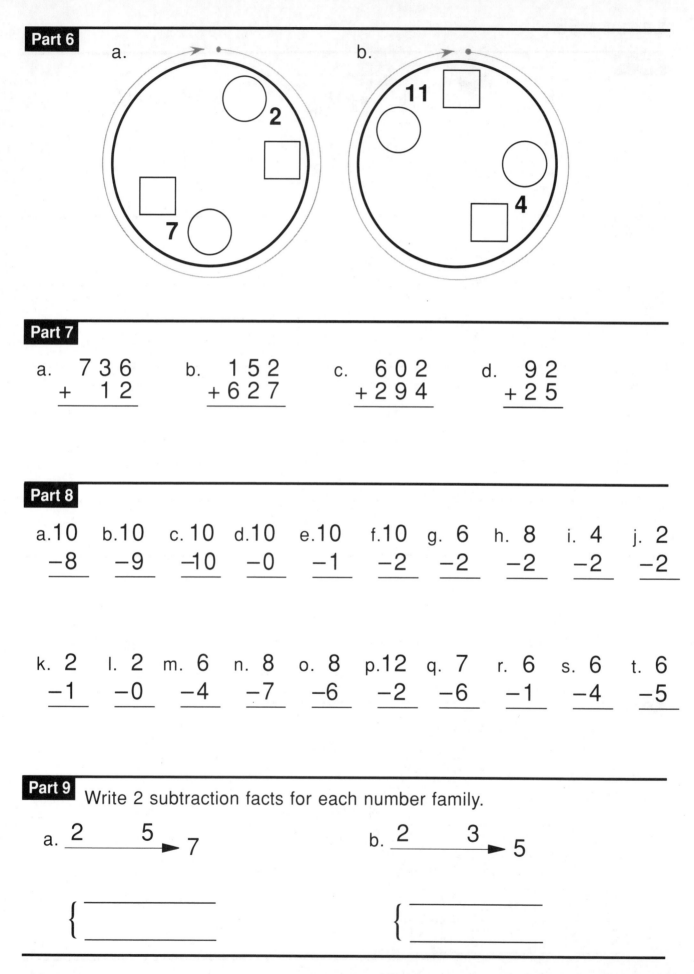

a.

b.

11

2

7

4

Part 7

a. 7 3 6
  + 1 2

b. 1 5 2
  + 6 2 7

c. 6 0 2
  + 2 9 4

d. 9 2
  + 2 5

Part 8

a. 10
  −8

b. 10
  −9

c. 10
  −10

d. 10
  −0

e. 10
  −1

f. 10
  −2

g. 6
  −2

h. 8
  −2

i. 4
  −2

j. 2
  −2

k. 2
  −1

l. 2
  −0

m. 6
  −4

n. 8
  −7

o. 8
  −6

p. 12
  −2

q. 7
  −6

r. 6
  −1

s. 6
  −4

t. 6
  −5

Part 9 Write 2 subtraction facts for each number family.

a. 2   5
         ➤ 7

b. 2   3
         ➤ 5

{ _____

{ _____

Lesson 59

Part 1

a. 10 + 5 = ___   e. 4 + 10 = ___   i. 10 + 5 = ___

b. 7 + 10 = ___   f. 10 + 7 = ___   j. 10 + 9 = ___

c. 10 + 2 = ___   g. 9 + 10 = ___   k. 2 + 10 = ___

d. 10 + 10 = ___   h. 10 + 1 = ___   l. 9 + 10 = ___

Part 2

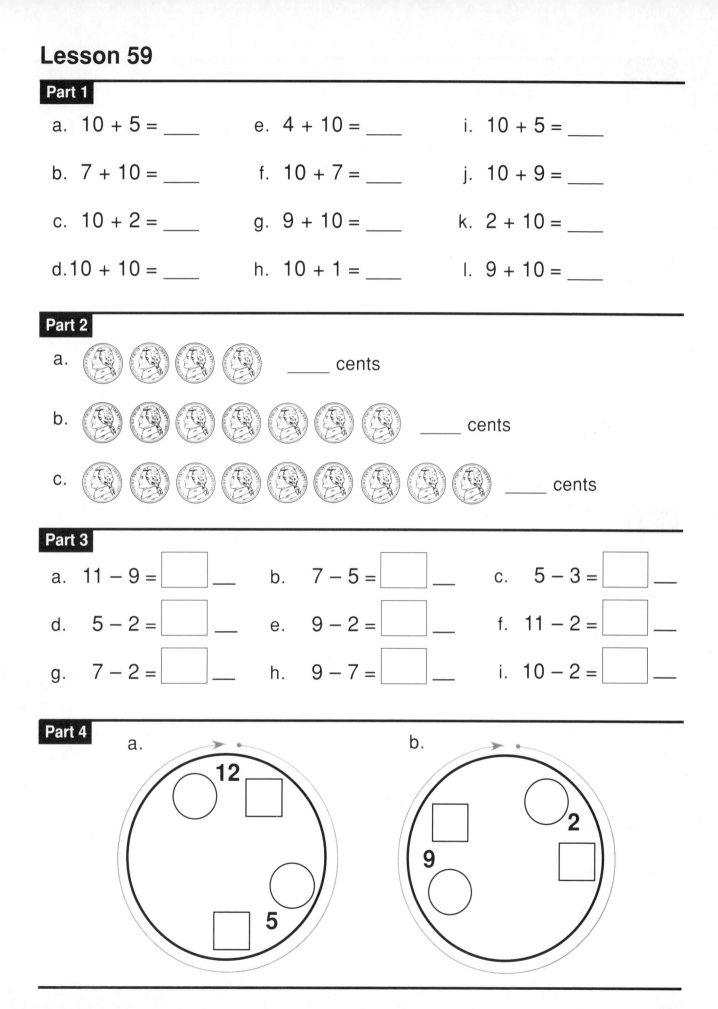

a. _____ cents

b. _____ cents

c. _____ cents

Part 3

a. 11 − 9 = ☐ __   b. 7 − 5 = ☐ __   c. 5 − 3 = ☐ __

d. 5 − 2 = ☐ __   e. 9 − 2 = ☐ __   f. 11 − 2 = ☐ __

g. 7 − 2 = ☐ __   h. 9 − 7 = ☐ __   i. 10 − 2 = ☐ __

Part 4

a.   12   5

b.   9   2

Part 5

a.

b.

c.

d.

Part 6

S	M	T	W	T	F	S
			1	2	3	4
5	6	7	8	9	10	11
12	13	14	15	16	17	18
19	20	21	22	23	24	25
26	27	28	29	30	31	

Part 7

a. 3 0 6

How many tens? ☐

How many hundreds? ☐

b. 7 9 4

How many tens? ☐

How many ones? ☐

c. 5 8 0

How many hundreds? ☐

How many ones? ☐

Part 8

a. 2 ___ 9 ___→ 11

Write two subtraction facts. { _____

_____

Part 9

a. 3 5 7
  + 2 1 2

b. 5 2 0
  + 2 7 4

c. 8 6
  + 1 1

d.   7 2
  + 8 1 2

Part 10

a. 5
−1

b. 8
−2

c. 4
−3

d. 4
−2

e. 8
−6

f. 6
−2

g. 7
−7

h. 4
−0

i. 10
−2

j. 6
−4

k. 4
−1

l. 3
−1

m. 7
−6

n. 10
−8

o. 8
−7

p. 11
−1

Lesson 60

Part 1

a. 6
  2
+ 1

b. 1
  8
+ 2

c. 2
  8
+ 1

d. 9
  2
+ 1

Part 2

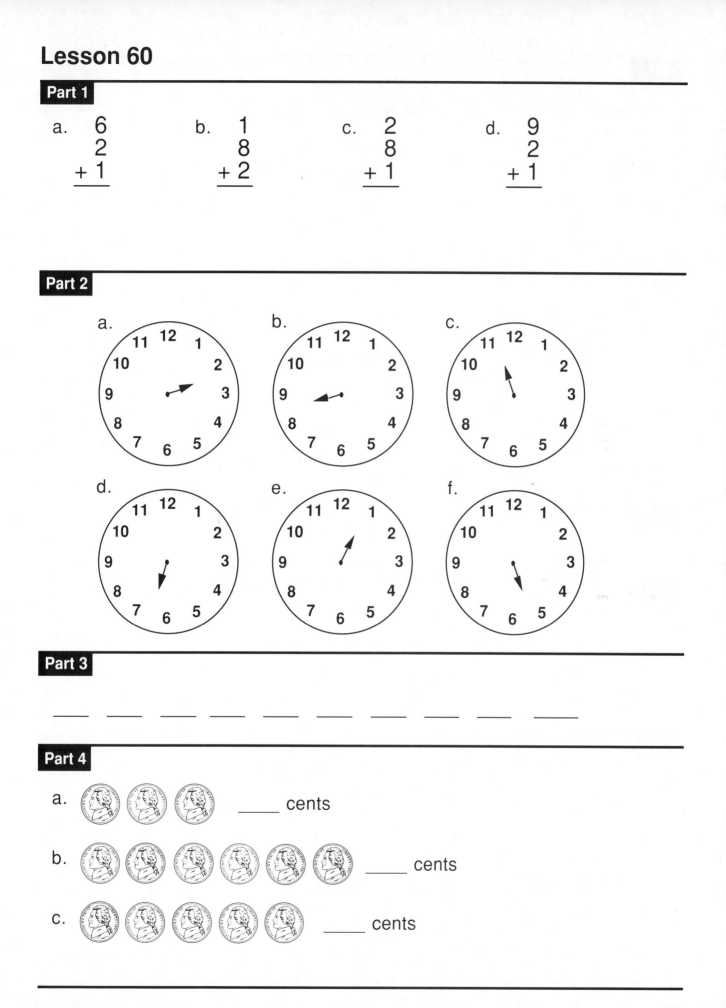

a.

b.

c.

d.

e.

f.

Part 3

— — — — — — — — —

Part 4

a. _____ cents

b. _____ cents

c. _____ cents

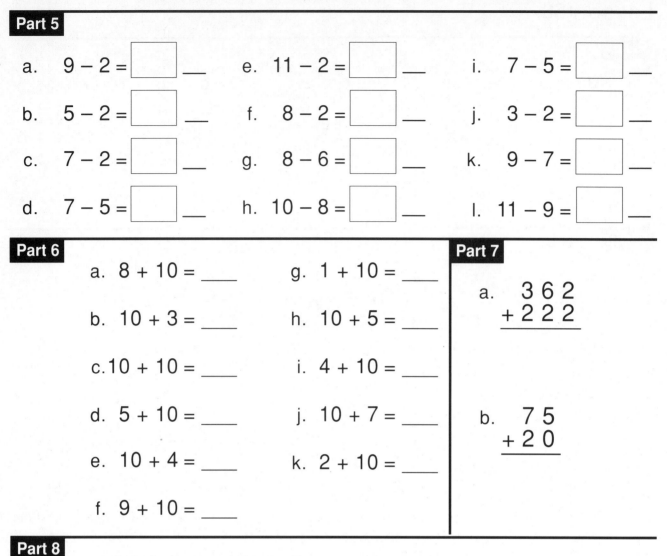

Part 5

a. 9 – 2 = ☐ __   e. 11 – 2 = ☐ __   i. 7 – 5 = ☐ __

b. 5 – 2 = ☐ __   f. 8 – 2 = ☐ __   j. 3 – 2 = ☐ __

c. 7 – 2 = ☐ __   g. 8 – 6 = ☐ __   k. 9 – 7 = ☐ __

d. 7 – 5 = ☐ __   h. 10 – 8 = ☐ __   l. 11 – 9 = ☐ __

Part 6

a. 8 + 10 = ____   g. 1 + 10 = ____

b. 10 + 3 = ____   h. 10 + 5 = ____

c. 10 + 10 = ____   i. 4 + 10 = ____

d. 5 + 10 = ____   j. 10 + 7 = ____

e. 10 + 4 = ____   k. 2 + 10 = ____

f. 9 + 10 = ____

Part 7

a.   3 6 2
  +2 2 2

b.   7 5
  +2 0

Part 8

a. Write all the numbers for counting by 2.

__ __ __ __ __ __ __ __ __ __

b. Write all the numbers for counting by 5.

__ __ __ __ __ __ __ __ __ __

Part 9

	First Day	Second Day	Third Day
Truck	380	270	403
Train	385	321	394
Horse	26	41	38

a. Train on second day? _____ miles

b. Horse on first day? _____ miles

c. Truck on first day? _____ miles

d. Train on third day? _____ miles

e. Circle the largest number in the train row.

f. Circle the smallest number in the third-day column.

Answers for Team Games

Lesson 16

a. 7 + 1 = 8 7 + 2 = 9	b. 5 + 1 = 6 5 + 2 = 7	c. 3 + 1 = 4 3 + 2 = 5
d. 9 + 1 = 10 9 + 2 = 11	e. 10 + 1 = 11 10 + 2 = 12	f. 4 + 1 = 5 4 + 2 = 6

Lesson 17

a. 5 + 1 = 6 5 + 2 = 7	b. 9 + 1 = 10 9 + 2 = 11	c. 1 + 1 = 2 1 + 2 = 3
d. 7 + 1 = 8 7 + 2 = 9	e. 3 + 1 = 4 3 + 2 = 5	f. 8 + 1 = 9 8 + 2 = 10

Lesson 18

a. 5 + 1 = 6 5 + 2 = 7	b. 25 + 1 = 26 25 + 2 = 27	c. 10 + 1 = 11 10 + 2 = 12
d. 1 + 1 = 2 1 + 2 = 3	e. 6 + 1 = 7 6 + 2 = 8	f. 4 + 1 = 5 4 + 2 = 6

Lesson 20

a. 6 + 1 = 7 6 + 2 = 8	b. 16 + 1 = 17 16 + 2 = 18	c. 8 + 1 = 9 8 + 2 = 10
d. 5 + 1 = 6 5 + 2 = 7	e. 9 + 1 = 10 9 + 2 = 11	f. 12 + 1 = 13 12 + 2 = 14

Lesson 22

a. 2 + 1 = 3 2 + 2 = 4	b. 7 + 1 = 8 7 + 2 = 9	c. 4 + 1 = 5 4 + 2 = 6
d. 5 + 1 = 6 5 + 2 = 7	e. 15 + 1 = 16 15 + 2 = 17	f. 10 + 1 = 11 10 + 2 = 12

Lesson 30

a. 2	c. 6	e. 8	g. 7	i. 3	k. 6	m. 5	o. 4
b. 5	d. 9	f. 10	h. 4	j. 7	l. 3	n. 9	p. 8

Lesson 36   Additional Fact Practice

a. $4 + 0 = 4$ e. $1 + 10 = 11$ i. $6 + 1 = 7$ m. $8 + 0 = 8$

b. $1 + 6 = 7$ f. $1 + 5 = 6$ j. $3 + 1 = 4$ n. $8 + 1 = 9$

c. $3 + 1 = 4$ g. $1 + 8 = 9$ k. $2 + 1 = 3$ o. $8 + 2 = 10$

d. $7 + 0 = 7$ h. $1 + 2 = 3$ l. $9 + 1 = 10$ p. $1 + 2 = 3$

Test Lesson 4

a.
$$\begin{array}{r} 4 \\ +1 \\ \hline 5 \end{array} \qquad \begin{array}{r} 4 \\ +2 \\ \hline 6 \end{array} \qquad \begin{array}{r} 4 \\ +3 \\ \hline 7 \end{array}$$

c.
$$\begin{array}{r} 5 \\ +1 \\ \hline 6 \end{array} \qquad \begin{array}{r} 5 \\ +2 \\ \hline 7 \end{array} \qquad \begin{array}{r} 5 \\ +3 \\ \hline 8 \end{array}$$

b.
$$\begin{array}{r} 7 \\ +1 \\ \hline 8 \end{array} \qquad \begin{array}{r} 7 \\ +2 \\ \hline 9 \end{array} \qquad \begin{array}{r} 7 \\ +3 \\ \hline 10 \end{array}$$

d.
$$\begin{array}{r} 9 \\ +1 \\ \hline 10 \end{array} \qquad \begin{array}{r} 9 \\ +2 \\ \hline 11 \end{array} \qquad \begin{array}{r} 9 \\ +3 \\ \hline 12 \end{array}$$

Lesson 41   Additional Fact Practice

a. $10 - 9 = 1$ e. $10 - 1 = 9$ i. $6 - 5 = 1$ m. $11 - 1 = 10$

b. $5 - 4 = 1$ f. $9 - 8 = 1$ j. $3 - 2 = 1$ n. $9 - 1 = 8$

c. $5 - 1 = 4$ g. $9 - 1 = 8$ k. $3 - 1 = 2$ o. $7 - 1 = 6$

d. $8 - 1 = 7$ h. $4 - 1 = 3$ l. $8 - 7 = 1$ p. $5 - 1 = 4$

Lesson 46   Additional Fact Practice

a. $2 + 8 = 10$ e. $10 + 2 = 12$ i. $2 + 6 = 8$ m. $6 + 2 = 8$

b. $2 + 4 = 6$ f. $6 + 2 = 8$ j. $8 + 2 = 10$ n. $2 + 2 = 4$

c. $2 + 2 = 4$ g. $4 + 2 = 6$ k. $10 + 2 = 12$ o. $2 + 10 = 12$

d. $2 + 6 = 8$ h. $2 + 2 = 4$ l. $2 + 4 = 6$ p. $8 + 2 = 10$

Lesson 50

a. $6 + 1 = 7$ f. $10 + 2 = 12$ j. $4 + 2 = 6$

b. $10 - 1 = 9$ g. $5 - 1 = 4$ k. $1 + 7 = 8$

c. $6 + 2 = 8$ h. $2 + 6 = 8$ l. $9 - 1 = 8$

d. $8 - 7 = 1$ i. $3 - 2 = 1$ m. $11 - 10 = 1$

e. $2 + 8 = 10$

Lesson 52

a. $\begin{array}{r} 5 \\ +1 \\ \hline 6 \end{array}$ b. $\begin{array}{r} 8 \\ -8 \\ \hline 0 \end{array}$ c. $\begin{array}{r} 2 \\ +8 \\ \hline 10 \end{array}$ d. $\begin{array}{r} 9 \\ -1 \\ \hline 8 \end{array}$ e. $\begin{array}{r} 6 \\ -5 \\ \hline 1 \end{array}$ f. $\begin{array}{r} 6 \\ +2 \\ \hline 8 \end{array}$ g. $\begin{array}{r} 3 \\ -1 \\ \hline 2 \end{array}$

h. $\begin{array}{r} 1 \\ +4 \\ \hline 5 \end{array}$ i. $\begin{array}{r} 6 \\ +0 \\ \hline 6 \end{array}$ j. $\begin{array}{r} 6 \\ -0 \\ \hline 6 \end{array}$ k. $\begin{array}{r} 9 \\ +1 \\ \hline 10 \end{array}$ l. $\begin{array}{r} 11 \\ -10 \\ \hline 1 \end{array}$ m. $\begin{array}{r} 3 \\ -0 \\ \hline 3 \end{array}$ n. $\begin{array}{r} 8 \\ +2 \\ \hline 10 \end{array}$

o. $\begin{array}{r} 8 \\ -1 \\ \hline 7 \end{array}$ p. $\begin{array}{r} 1 \\ +7 \\ \hline 8 \end{array}$ q. $\begin{array}{r} 5 \\ -5 \\ \hline 0 \end{array}$ r. $\begin{array}{r} 4 \\ -3 \\ \hline 1 \end{array}$ s. $\begin{array}{r} 2 \\ -1 \\ \hline 1 \end{array}$ t. $\begin{array}{r} 4 \\ +2 \\ \hline 6 \end{array}$

Lesson 53

a. 6
−2
4

b. 7
+0
7

c. 7
+1
8

d. 10
−8
2

e. 4
−2
2

f. 0
+8
8

g. 2
+8
10

h. 6
−4
2

i. 7
−6
1

j. 2
+4
6

k. 10
−8
2

l. 7
−7
0

m. 1
+8
9

n. 5
+1
6

o. 2
+10
12

p. 8
−2
6

q. 9
−0
9

r. 8
+2
10

s. 1
+4
5

t. 2
+2
4

Lesson 56   Additional Fact Practice

a. $8 - 6 = 2$ e. $4 - 2 = 2$ i. $6 - 1 = 5$ m. $10 - 9 = 1$

b. $10 - 8 = 2$ f. $10 - 2 = 8$ j. $6 - 0 = 6$ n. $7 - 6 = 1$

c. $4 - 4 = 0$ g. $8 - 2 = 6$ k. $10 - 0 = 10$ o. $6 - 6 = 0$

d. $4 - 3 = 1$ h. $6 - 2 = 4$ l. $10 - 1 = 9$ p. $6 - 5 = 1$